Advance Praise for *SQ21*

Scholars

"Cindy Wigglesworth has devised an assessment that is an excellent overview of the process of general spiritual intelligence itself, including developmental variables—and thus one I can highly recommend!"

Ken Wilber
author of A Brief History of Everything, founder of Integral Institute

"Between moral reasoning and ego development, there is a Twilight Zone of passion, energy, openness, and mindfulness to all around us. It is precisely in this realm that Cindy Wigglesworth has ventured to pioneer new ground in our relationship to larger forces—our spiritual selves. She inspires using a cognitive behavioral approach in expanding our spiritual awareness. This book is a must-read for anyone on a quest to find new meaning in life and work, but a survival issue for those of us feeling lost or in a mid-life crisis!"

Richard Boyatzis
Distinguished University Professor, Case Western Reserve University,
co-author of Primal Leadership and Resonant Leadership

"Spiritual intelligence as a concept is not entirely new, but it has not been clearly explicated or mined for its full potential until now. Cindy Wigglesworth does for spiritual intelligence what Daniel Goleman does for emotional intelligence in giving it a clear definition, a sharpened focus, and elucidating the difference it can make in organizations as well as in individuals. While so many writers on 'spiritual' topics put forth vague platitudes that offer nothing concrete to the real world of business and institutions, Wigglesworth uses her decades of corporate experience and her significant knowledge of adult development and organizational process to present in this book a virtual manifesto for the benefits of—and need for—spiritual intelligence. Wigglesworth is the one person who makes spiritual intelligence both spiritual and intelligent. This book will be the singular, defining work in this field for years to come."

Jill Carroll, Ph.D.
Scholar, writer, and speaker in Religious Studies

Business Leaders and Experts

"Cindy Wigglesworth's content is consistently world-class quality, thought-pro-voking, and fresh. She has the unique ability to manage the polarization required of a top class business book—edgy but practical; stimulating but rel-evant; complex but simple. Cindy was a key player in the design, develop-ment, and delivery of a quality Executive Leadership Program at BHP Billiton Petroleum—our top 100 leaders gave her full marks on every dimension of effectiveness. They left the program ready to make a difference—and that's what Cindy does—she makes a difference."

David Nelson
Vice President of Human Resources, BHP Billiton Petroleum

"Finally, an intelligent book on Spiritual Intelligence! Cindy Wigglesworth doesn't just preach its value, but shows us how it can be measured and developed as a skill-set. And what's more, she does so in clear, pragmatic, and accessible terms, avoiding both New Age vagueness and religious dogma. SQ21 is a must-read for anyone trying to navigate the multidimen-sional challenges of life today."

Patricia Aburdene
bestselling author of Megatrends 2010

"Having met Cindy, it comes as little surprise that I also want to spend more time with her book. A quick read was enticing—now, to savor a slow one. Few things are as exhilarating as to learn you can develop new powers."

Steve Leveen
CEO & Co-Founder, Levenger

"With great clarity, Cindy lays out the pathway to wisdom. SQ21 is a must read for anyone who aspires to be a true leader."

Richard Barrett
author of The New Leadership Paradigm

"A real heart-opener. The skills recommended in this book will advance behav-iors that provide a sense of comfort and peace both inside and out. All of your relationships will be impacted and the joy of life enhanced."

Douglas D. Hawthorne, FACHE
Chief Executive Officer, Texas Health Resources

"Cindy is a no-nonsense businessperson, an innovative researcher, and an excellent coach. She has captured beautifully what people think privately about religion and spirituality, and provided us all with valuable tools with which we can express ourselves and grow. Her common sense, experience, and research provide a framework she calls Spiritual Intelligence—and the result is powerful. This is the next step beyond emotional intelligence. I believe her SQ21 skills will define those who can truly claim to be 'Higher Ground Leaders.'"

Lance Secretan
Founder & CEO, The Secretan Center Inc., Author of *Higher Ground*

"Cindy Wigglesworth has described a new frontier of human potential. Spiritual Intelligence, as she has defined it, is a vital resource for our businesses, our communities, and our society. This book defines that resource and gives us the opportunity to cultivate and expand the human spirit."

Bryan Welch
Publisher, *Mother Earth News, Utne Reader,*
author of *Beautiful and Abundant: Building the World We Want*

"Spiritual intelligence is your ability to bring embodied insight of your true nature to your life, relationships, and career. I work with CEOs all over the world and I see firsthand how a difference between realizing one's dreams and feeling unfulfilled is the degree of spiritual intelligence leaders embody in their lives."

Robb Smith
CEO, Integral Institute

"*SQ21: The Twenty-One Skills of Spiritual Intelligence* is a must-read for health care leaders who have tried every financial, marketing, organizational development, and customer service strategy and continue to fail to create an environment where staff can flourish and patients are happy and healing. The book's evidence and experiential base provides one of the missing links in strategy and explains how all leaders, from the front lines to the C-suite, must evolve in order to create cultures of excellence with outcomes to match. Cindy Wigglesworth describes how people who aspire to become great leaders must seek to connect with a higher purpose and tap into not only their PQ, IQ and EQ, but also their SQ as a powerful source of guidance, direction and meaning. The SQ21 Assessment, used as a development tool, can identify opportunities for growth in individuals, teams, and cultures, and provide a pathway for not only improved organizational performance, but meaning in everyday work."

Pamela Klauer Triolo, PhD, RN, FAAN
Former Chief Nursing Executive and Senior Vice President,
The Methodist Health System, Houston, TX
Former System Chief Nursing Officer, UPMC, Pittsburgh, PA

"Become intelligent about spirit. SQ21 unlocks the process of spiritual intelligence and renders it actionable. Cindy's discoveries demonstrate how we can all be higher expressions of ourselves and be even more fully human."

Kevin Clark
author of *Brandscendence*, President & Founder, Content Evolution

"Cindy Wigglesworth worked with me while I was CEO of The Methodist Health Care System in Houston. Together with other internal leaders, we initiated and effected a successful culture change to live up to our goal of 'a spiritual environment of caring.' This culture change was rooted in our mission, vision and our 'I CARE' values (Integrity, Compassion, Accountability, Respect and Excellence). Cindy's faith-neutral and yet faith-friendly approach to spiritual topics allowed us to embody respect for our employees who are of many faith traditions. Her experience with what it takes to create a systemic culture change allowed us to design and implement a process to make a sustained difference in our culture—one that got us on the Fortune 100 Best Employers list and keeps us there today. SQ is a valuable approach to putting spirituality back into your company in a practical way and Cindy is a change-agent who understands a CEO's perspective."

Ron Girotto
CEO (retired), The Methodist Health Care System, Houston, Texas

Spiritual Leaders

"Human beings are bio-psycho-socio-spiritual beings. Cindy Wigglesworth has put real substance to the psycho/spiritual dynamics of becoming human or becoming whole. In so doing, this study integrates all four cornerstones of our humanity in a most systematic way. This is a great contribution to the most important conversation of the 21st Century."

J. Pittman McGehee, D.D.
Author of *The Invisible Church: Finding Spirituality Where You Are*

"From the first moment I discovered Cindy Wigglesworth's work in 2003, I've been absolutely convinced that her Spiritual Intelligence model would completely 'evolutionize' a person's spiritual development. SQ21 is an important book for those who are seeking spiritual mastery as our world becomes increasingly complex in the twenty-first century. I highly recommend it to spiritual seekers everywhere!"

Susan M. Beck
Former Chief Operating Officer, Association of Unity Churches International

"At a time when deep spirituality is desperately needed and yet widely misunderstood, Cindy Wigglesworth has provided a brilliant map that clearly shows us the way. Her wise, accessible, personal, and often funny book teaches us that spirituality is an innate human intelligence that can be developed through a commitment to a program of 'spiritual weightlifting.' When practiced with the humility of adventure, Cindy's guidance will bring profound and lasting change in every aspect of your life, making you more compassionate, peaceful, effective, and happy so that you may be the needed change-agent for our evolving world."

Rabbi Alan Lurie
Author of *Five Minutes on Mondays: Finding Unexpected Peace, Purpose, and Fulfillment at Work*

"*SQ21* bridges the inner work of spiritual life with the practical dimensions. The challenges of our time require deep commitments to ultimate values, as well as the practical skills to implement them. Based on years of research and experience, this book will be extremely valuable for leaders, educators, coaches, and consultants seeking an effective, pragmatic, and holistic way to embrace spirituality."

Diane Musho Hamilton
Zen Priest and Teacher

"Cindy Wigglesworth leads you on a 21-step journey into new levels of spiritual understanding, and by the time it's over, has orchestrated a gradual leap into the deep domain of conscious living."

Howard Caesar
Senior Minister, Unity Church of Christianity

"More than just a book—a lovely and practical way to evolve spirituality. Filled with tested practices, in depth insights, and helpful stories, Cindy reveals her own journey and takes us on an accelerated voyage of our own."

Paul Smith
Author of *Integral Christianity: The Spirit's Call to Evolve*

SQ21

SQ21

THE TWENTY-ONE SKILLS OF SPIRITUAL INTELLIGENCE

Cindy Wigglesworth

SelectBooks, Inc.
New York

SQ21 is a trademark of Conscious Pursuits, Inc.

This edition published by SelectBooks, Inc.

For information address SelectBooks, Inc., New York, New York.

First Edition

ISBN 978-1-59079-235-3

Library of Congress Cataloging-in-Publication Data
Wigglesworth, Cindy.
    SQ21: the twenty-one skills of spiritual intelligence / Cindy Wigglesworth. – 1st ed.
p. cm.
Summary : "Business owner of successful consulting company presents a pragmatic approach to spiritual development by identifying twenty-one measurable spiritual intelligence skills described in faith-neutral terms. Author relates her coaching work with businesspeople, spiritual and religious leaders, coaches, and educators to validate the SQ21 spiritual intelligence assessment instrument she pioneered for people to understand and increase their spiritual intelligence"—Provided by publisher.
Includes bibliographical references (p.   ) and index.
ISBN 978-1-59079-235-3 (hardbound book : alk. paper)
1. Spiritual intelligence. I. Title.
BL629.5.S65W54 2012
204–dc23
                                    2012005106

Book design by Kathleen Isaksen

Manufactured in the United States of America
10 9 8 7 6 5 4 3 2 1

CONTENTS

"To exist is to change,
to change is to mature,
to mature is to go on creating oneself endlessly."

—Henri Bergson, *Creative Evolution*

ACKNOWLEDGMENTS

As with any endeavor of this size, there are a lot of people to thank, including you, the reader, for whom this book exists. Thank you for picking up this book and being willing to consider its contents.

For my family, I have a few special acknowledgements. For being a wonderful spouse and encouraging me during this time, I thank my husband, Bill Wigglesworth. I couldn't have done it without his faith and support. He put up with me talking about SQ and all related topics in ways only someone who loves you deeply can do. Bill keeps me grounded in what matters and is a lot of fun to hang around with. He is a wonderful "co-parent" to our kids and grandkids, who always are our highest priority.

Many thanks go to my daughter, Jessica, to my stepson, Logan, and my stepdaughter, Jamie. As a parent and stepparent one gets stretched in all the "right ways." I have had chances to see my weaknesses—and acknowledge and work on them. Hopefully, more often than not, I have shifted out of my ego and operated from Higher Self. I always say the goal isn't 100% of the time—that would be sainthood. But getting as close as I can would be good!

My good friend, Dr. Jill Carroll, deserves thanks on several fronts. As an expert in world religions and former Executive Director of the Boniuk Center for Religious Tolerance at Rice University, she has been a powerful help to me as I worked to create a faith-neutral yet faith-friendly approach to developing spiritual intelligence. As a fellow entrepreneur, public speaker, teacher, and writer, she understands my world better than almost anyone else I know. She has a wonderful cut-to-the-chase approach to things—asking powerful questions where they need to be asked.

My family of origin provided the ground for my life-launch and many of my drives to learn stem from there. Much love and thanks to my parents, Chuck and Marjorie Sitter, and to my sister, Dianna, and brother, Doug. Relationships of such length and depth provide so much for us to learn and appreciate. I am deeply grateful to each of you.

Creating the SQ21 would not have been possible without help from experts. Specifically, I want to thank the following people. At Customer Value Systems, Dr. Brant Wilson and his business partner Joan E. Jones, both of whom worked with me to flesh out the assessment. We worked through each of the 21 skills, with me describing what I thought it demanded. How could it be observed? How could it be described? Joan and Brant helped me create "psychometrically sound" survey questions. In terms of research work, they oversaw the focus groups, the alpha and beta testing, and the initial reliability studies. With great patience, they helped me think through the scoring algorithm, and found the programmers who built the software that now does the complex scoring and reporting for the SQ21. We continue to work together as we run analyses and improve the SQ21. Rick Sline created and maintains the current version of the software. He does so with humor, grace, and deep competence. Dr. Michael McElhenie used his experience with EQ studies to help design and supervise the construct (criterion) validation study. And my friend Dr. Susanne Cook-Greuter kindly assisted in the cross-correlation of my SQ21 tool with her adult development/leadership development tool—the highly respected SCTi/MAP.

The community of coaches and consultants, therapists, religious and spiritual leaders, and others who have been drawn to get certified in this assessment are an inspiring group of people. Certification allows our SQ21 coaches to debrief the SQ21 with their clients. We have trained well over 150 people at this point—and the number grows monthly. It is a source of great joy for me to be in connection with such dedicated people. They expand the possibility of this work every day. They take it beyond where any one person could have imagined it might go. To each of you, a deep bow. Thank you for your commitment to being agents of love and evolution.

Of course, no office runs itself. Amy Barney Alston was with me, first as our nanny and then as office manager and friend, from the first day of incorporation of my business until she got married in 2010. In 2010 Gabi Dedmon McLeod assumed responsibility for trying to keep me, and the office, organized. Both of these women are deeply spiritually intelligent themselves—and model both worldly and divine grace. Ladies, I couldn't have done this without you—thank you.

In the mechanics of writing this book, I owe the greatest thanks to Ellen Daly. Ellen interviewed me, talked with me, had my various classes and speeches transcribed. She helped me organize my thoughts for this book. Together we drafted outlines and key points. She often compiled a first draft of a chapter by pulling from the interviews and other resources, making it easier for me to take it and shape it. She also gently nagged me to keep things moving along. I am indebted to Ellen for "getting into my head" so effectively and keeping this project moving, including the less fun details like working with me on the index. Laura Didyk did a thorough and careful copyedit to bring the manuscript to its final state.

SelectBooks has been a fabulous publisher to work with. Thanks to Bill Gladstone, my agent, and to his friend Kenzi Sugihara of SelectBooks for your confidence in me and in this book.

After leaving my former denomination, my desire to learn a more practical form of spirituality was supported and nurtured inside Unity's worldcentric, inclusive, expansive network of teachers, workshops, churches, and communities. Unity of North Houston (my former community) and Unity of Houston (my current community led by Rev. Howard Caesar) have my gratitude for providing a "where" to go to for fellowship, learning, and friendship with like-minded souls. And beyond Houston, I thank all my friends at Unity worldwide for your inspirational examples and teachings.

Finally, my deep gratitude goes out to the thought-leaders who have most strongly influenced me. I would like to thank Richard Boyatzis and Daniel Goleman for their work on Emotional Intelligence—your work was seminal for me. Other great people who have influenced my thinking as I created this SQ21 assessment and improved on it, and as I wrote this book, include: M. Scott Peck, Abraham Maslow, Ken Wilber, James Fowler, Susanne Cook-Greuter, Robert Kegan, and Howard Gardner. Rev. Pittman McGehee has served as my personal mentor, coach, and

Jungian therapist for many years now—thank you so much for your depth of knowledge and the wisdom of its transmission.

My debt goes even further to the myriad people who work in the field of positive psychology, adult development, leadership development, personal and spiritual growth, brain science, new physics, and future studies. And to the British Romantic poets and the American Transcendentalists—you touched my soul deeply in my twenties and the influence lingers. Among faith traditions, I like to call myself "a Zen Christian," which is to say, Christian with Buddhist and Taoist influences. I would go further and say that all the great mystics and sages, from Rumi to Jesus, from Krishnamurti to the Dalai Lama, have contributed to the body of knowledge and inspiration on which I draw and am nourished. No one of us can take the "next step" without building upon the countless brilliant and courageous people who preceded us. To all my teachers—of all generations—I thank you.

INTRODUCTION

"Love your neighbor as you love yourself." Sounds good. But am I really supposed to love *him?* You don't mean *her,* do you?

This is how my spiritual journey began. I was seeking practical steps to achieve what seemed like a very idealistic goal. Raised Roman Catholic, I deeply admired people who seemed to embody love—Jesus, Mother Teresa, and other saints. Later, I added holy people from many faiths to this list, people who seemed able to love others well—Gandhi, Buddha, and many more. But it seemed impossible for me. I asked myself: "How can an ordinary person like me learn how to stop being impatient, judgmental, and occasionally cranky? How can I love other unreasonable and cranky people?"

As a teen, I was very discouraged by this line of thought. It seemed that what I learned in church was setting me up for failure. I felt doomed to be eternally inadequate. I prayed for guidance from a God I only sort of believed in—as in "God, if you are there. . . ." Then, one day I heard a "voice" in my head, asking in a sympathetic tone, "What exactly do you want?" And a wiser part of me answered without me "thinking" about it: "I want to be wise. I want to understand." I felt some peace settle over me. That felt good: wisdom.

There's a saying: *be careful what you ask for.* For me, wisdom would be a hard-won treasure. It came to me in small pieces. Each piece has been precious and wonderful—and has typically cost me something. Sometimes it came with some external pressure and difficulty. Mostly it came with internal pain—the pain of releasing attachment to my own ideas of the "one-right-way" to do or be. I had to let go of pieces of my immature ego in exchange for each piece of wisdom. And I am certainly not done learning.

I am not one of those people who had a near-death experience or a moment of revelation and came out of it feeling an unbroken sense of connection to the Divine. My connections have been sporadic, and my moments of insight have been won mostly through hard work on my part, matched by gifts of grace.

My husband, Bill, likes to say that the best basketball coaches were not typically the best players. Gifted players often seem to "just know" how to handle the ball, move through the opposing team, or land a lay-up. The best coaches typically struggled as players. They had to drill and practice to get their free throws right. They had to study the formations and watch hours of recorded game plays to get the feel for where to be on the floor. They made up, with effort, for what other more natural players seemed to "just know." And they make good coaches because they can show others the slow and steady way to practice and drill the skills. Bill says this to encourage me as I work on myself and as I seek to help others on the path. I believe that I am able to coach others because I had to work hard to learn what I have learned.

Mine has been the path of the slow and the steady. And it was because of my own quest to live from love and act from wisdom that I devised a way of describing the skills I have been trying all my life to build. I built the mental map that I needed and that I hope you will find helpful as well.

Specifically, this 21 Skills model is the result of asking this question: *I want to be a good person—where do I start?* I started with the spiritual figures I deeply admired: How could I be as loving as Jesus? Be peaceful and nonviolent like Gandhi? Keep my center and stay wise and strong in the face of terrible things like the Dalai Lama? Have vision and faith like Nelson Mandela?

I knew I had a lot of work to do on myself. But how could I know what to study or work on next? Fellow seekers all raved about different books, processes, retreats, teachers, and workshops. How could I know what I personally needed next?

For years, I used my intuition and advice from friends to help me answer those questions. I consumed materials at a pace that matched the intensity of my college studies. Yet I felt that I "wasted" a lot of time on what seemed to be dead ends. Eventually, I saw a pattern emerging that, over time, evolved into the 21 Skills.

While I was reading, attending workshops, and practicing various techniques, I noticed that an improvement was occurring in my relationships at work and at home. As I was reducing my ego-activation, I was becoming a better human being, a nicer person. This "stuff" I was working so hard on clearly had value that transcended my own personal happiness. I was becoming a better mother, wife, friend, teammate, and a more effective leader.

The idea for describing Spiritual Intelligence as the practical path to releasing ego and learning to love others grew slowly—until it solidified one day into the concept of describing it as a series of skills. I discovered Daniel Goleman's and Richard Boyatzis' work on Emotional Intelligence and immediately loved it. I realized that just as relationship skills can be broken down into the eighteen skills of Emotional Intelligence (which Goleman and Boyatzis call "competencies"), Spiritual Intelligence consists of parallel skills that could enable wisdom and loving behaviors.

What if I could name those Spiritual Intelligence skills and describe them on a spectrum from "novice" to "expert"? Could a framework of skills and levels of development help me and others know what to work on next?

In 2000 I left a great job at Exxon[1] to answer these questions. Having been in human resources my whole career, I knew that spirituality was an incredibly diversity-sensitive topic. Whatever I created would need to be faith-neutral and yet faith-friendly. For example, I would want language that agnostics and atheists could connect with as well—clear definitions and a glossary of synonyms would be crucial.

I was in the midst of creating the first version of the assessment when the September 11, 2001, terrorist attacks occurred. The aftermath included a great deal of interreligious tension. It made the need to find a common language with which to talk about spiritual topics even more urgent in my mind. It was clear to me that if we confused our desire to be spiritual with more egoic needs to be "right" and be on the "only correct path," then we would keep on killing each other. We needed a way to honor other spiritual paths (including secular ones) through the understanding of our commonalities. At the same time I wanted to honor the fact that for some people, there is a sincere belief that there is "one right path for me"—whether that path is Buddhism, Hinduism, Islam, Christianity, or something else.

Hopelessly idealistic? Perhaps. But I like the advice I heard once as a young person: shoot for the stars and maybe you'll catch the moon. So the SQ21 assessment, and this book, are my best efforts at shooting for the stars. I hope the result will be catching the moon, as I offer what I hope is an important piece of the next evolutionary step for humanity: developing our Spiritual Intelligence. Spiritual Intelligence, as distinct from both spirituality and religion, is a set of skills we develop over time, with practice.

In this book, you will see the results of decades of inquiry and twelve years of very focused effort. As you read, please keep in mind two important points:

First, my goal is to outline the skills for Spiritual Intelligence—*but not prescribe the path you "must" use to develop them.* Once you examine the skills and consider which skill you want to focus on, you can return to your path of choice (your religion, or spiritual or secular practice) and find tools within that path specific to the skill.

Second, *with the 21 Skills in mind, you can zero in on what will help you right now.* I hope this will increase your satisfaction and the speed with which you can grow and develop.

My specific hope for you is that the 21 Skills of SQ will create a really helpful roadmap and diagnostic—a way for you to save time and effort. You can read these chapters and see what skills resonate for you. Then you can focus your efforts on finding tools, workshops, and practices that will help you build the skills you want within your path of choice. If you are so inclined, you might decide to take the SQ21 assessment (available at DeepChange.com) and engage a trained coach to help you discover new insights.

My largest, bravest hope for this work is that Spiritual Intelligence will help us as a species "grow up" and better navigate our complex, interdependent world. I hope that a positive tipping point is reached when enough of us find our way to loving our neighbors and ourselves, to focusing on what is highest and best, and thereby lead ourselves into a better future for humanity. And if the SQ21 can be one small piece of that, I will be delighted.

Blessings to you and to all of us. May we all build the spiritual muscle we need to become the best people we can.

And thereby, may we build a beautiful future for humanity.

Cindy Wigglesworth
Houston, Texas, 2012

PART ONE
What Is Spiritual Intelligence?

ONE

Becoming Fully Human

*"Man cannot approach the divine by reaching
beyond the human; he can approach Him through
becoming human. To become human is what he,
this individual man, has been created for."*

—Martin Buber, *Hasidism and Modern Man* (1956)

Becoming fully human is a great adventure—one that requires us to grow and stretch ourselves. Do you, too, feel the call to grow? Some of us go through childhood with this yearning. Others discover that restless self later in life. If you have picked up this book, I suspect you are on the move. You are someone who wants to become more fully human—to be the best YOU that you can be. Once this hunger awakens, no distractions, purchases, or promotions at work will satisfy it. You just know there is "something more."

Transcending our "smaller nature" and growing into our full potential as human beings is the most important and fulfilling thing we can do with our lives. The set of skills that I collectively call "Spiritual Intelligence" are designed to help you to become more fully who you are, to continue to grow and develop, and to live with greater consciousness, direction, wisdom, and compassion. These skills and the larger goal of becoming fully human are in alignment with all the world's great wisdom traditions. Psychologist Abraham Maslow described this as "a single ultimate goal for mankind, a far goal toward which all persons strive . . . [which] amounts to realizing the potentialities of the person, that is to say, becoming fully human."

We are drawn toward our own higher potential; we are seeking something. Yet we usually cannot describe the discontent we feel or how we would go about reaching the place we are trying to "get to." Even the experts—the mystics, teachers, saints, and sages from the great wisdom traditions—don't seem to agree when it comes down to the nuts and bolts of spiritual transformation. As Maslow points out, there are numerous names for this "ultimate goal"—self-actualization, self-transcendence, spiritual realization or awakening, individuation, and many more. And there are many paths to get there. Each culture and faith tradition has its own path and some faiths seem convinced that the way they describe is the only true one. This tendency to be exclusive and to make other paths wrong has troubled me for most of my life. If there truly is a "single ultimate goal" for human development, should it not be possible to describe a faith-neutral and objective way to reach that goal? Through using tools pioneered by psychology and other sciences we can create and refine a statistically reliable system by which progress in the spiritual dimension of human development can be measured. Within such a structure each spiritual path can continue to teach its adherents how to grow, and yet we can show that many other paths can work also.

What I offer in this book is a way to describe a previously missing piece of the puzzle regarding how we become fully human—how we live up to our highest potential. It is based on and expands upon pre-existing work in the field of multiple intelligences. By expanding the field to include Spiritual Intelligence we can move beyond the "who is right and who is wrong" conversation. We can focus on the goal, and can each choose our own path to get there. By using the 21 Skills of Spiritual Intelligence you can assess where you are, plan out some concrete steps for growth, and quickly begin to see impact in areas of life that matter to you.

Defining Our Goal

Let's begin with a question: Whom do you admire as a spiritual leader? Think about this for a moment. The word "admire" is key. Think about those people who come to mind, without hesitation, as being examples of living a distinctly noble life. And then ask yourself a second question:

Why do I admire these people as spiritual leaders? What are the traits that make them stand out as exemplars of higher human potential? You may want to take a moment to write down your list of noble people and their traits.

I have asked these questions to thousands of people from many different walks of life and a variety of spiritual or religious persuasions—from devoted believers to avowed atheists. What I find both reassuring and fascinating is when asked this simple question we agree much more than one might expect.

The names that come up are fairly consistent and tend to fall into predictable categories: major religious figures such as Abraham, Buddha, the Dalai Lama, Gandhi, Jesus, Lord Krishna, Mohammed, Moses, Mother Teresa, the Pope, and various saints; great political leaders, peace activists, or freedom fighters, such as Jimmy Carter, Gandhi, Martin Luther King, Jr., Nelson Mandela, and Thich Nhat Hanh (some of whom are also spiritual/religious leaders); prominent cultural figures and television personalities such as Deepak Chopra or Oprah Winfrey; fictional characters, like Yoda from *Star Wars,* or *To Kill A Mockingbird's* Atticus Finch; and various relatives, local or current religious or spiritual teachers, guidance counselors or school teachers, friends or sometimes even a boss, who inspire us in our day-to-day lives.

More importantly, when people are asked to describe the particular *traits* that cause them to admire these people, the words that come back are strikingly similar. Beyond religious and cultural differences, we do in fact have quite clear and remarkably congruent ideas about what higher human attainment looks like. Here are some of the descriptors that I hear most often regarding spiritual leaders. He or she:

- Is authentic and has integrity
- Is calm, peaceful, and centered
- Has a clear mission or vocation
- Is compassionate, caring, kind, and loving
- Is courageous, dependable, faithful and faith-filled
- Is forgiving and generous
- Is a great leader, teacher, and/or mentor
- Is humble, inspiring, and wise

- Is nonviolent
- Is open-minded and open-hearted
- Is persistent, values-driven, and committed to serving others.

While the words chosen may vary slightly for a given person or group, they tend to be synonyms of the words in this list. What the consistency of the responses tells me is that we already have a general perception of what makes someone worthy of our admiration and possibly our emulation. *We recognize a fuller, higher expression of humanity when we see one.* When we put aside our ideas about what spirituality means, or the preconceptions about religion that may be lodged in our minds from childhood, we find that we have a natural "spiritual compass." We know what nobility looks like. And the restlessness we feel is the feeling of being drawn towards to the full expression of our own human potential.

The question that then remains, is: How do we get there? How do we move from where we are today to being more like Gandhi, Jesus, Nelson Mandela, the Dalai Lama, or the wise teacher who inspired us as a child? While we have an innate sense of where we need to go, most of us have not been taught the specific skills and abilities we are trying to attain when we seek spiritual growth. Nor have we had any means of measuring where we are on the journey toward developing these skills. These are the areas to which this book hopes to contribute.

I am not offering yet another alternative path or claiming that my path is better than all the others. Rather, I am taking an altogether different approach—one that can be applied to whatever particular path you are on, and make that path more effective, more deliberate, and more clearly transformative. This approach is the cultivation of what I call "Spiritual Intelligence."

What Is Spiritual Intelligence?

Spiritual Intelligence, or "SQ" as it is often abbreviated, is my field of specialization. In the next chapter we will look at how it relates to the other kinds of intelligence that we may be more familiar with and spend some time unpacking the notion of multiple intelligences in general. But by way of an introduction to this field, I would like to share with you how I came to it. When my journey began I knew nothing about multiple intelligence theory or even the now widely accepted notion of Emotional Intelligence. I was simply a human resources professional working in a large oil company in Texas, and was sensitive to my own growth and the effects this had on my capacity as a leader.

In my mid-thirties, I noticed that I was becoming far more impactful as a leader than I had been before. I was getting multimillion dollar projects approved quickly (quite a feat in the 1990s in human resources). Managers were quick to help me staff my projects, even as their own projects were under-resourced. And my teams were flourishing, creative, and productive. I traced the development of these powerful new leadership skills back to the spiritual work that I was doing at the time. I had been focusing on reducing my attachment to my own egoic needs and putting my attention instead on the greater good of the team, the customers, the company, and beyond. As I shifted my focus in this way, I could see solutions I'd been previously blind to and work with people in creative ways that would never have occurred to me before. It was obvious to me that my own spiritual growth was directly impacting my effectiveness as a leader. However, I knew that talking about spirituality would not be very welcome in the corporate environment. As a human resources manager, I understood all too well the potential sensitivity of bringing anything that sounded remotely like religion into the workplace—especially in Texas, where many people are of a conservative Christian orientation and intense theological debates could be easily sparked. This was when I first began to consider how the new capacities and potentials I was discovering could be translated into universal terms that were free from religious baggage.

Later, I came to hypothesize that there should be specific "skills" or competencies that could be identified as contributing to SQ, and even ways to measure these skills scientifically. Finding that no one had as yet created this language, I left Exxon after twenty years, walking away from a successful career to launch into the unknown. I started my own company and set out to define SQ and to test my hypothesis.

My core questions were: can we create a rigorously tested, faithneutral, professional quality instrument for measuring this powerful skill-set? And will this skill-set indeed show relationship to human development and leadership capacities?

The biggest obstacle I faced in my days at Exxon, and still face with many clients today, is the concern about respecting religious diversity. Let me assure you, then, if you share these concerns, that Spiritual Intelligence is distinct from spirituality or religion. In order to begin this book with clarity around these key distinctions, here are my definitions of spirituality, religion, and finally, Spiritual Intelligence.

Spirituality, as I define it, is *the innate human need to be connected to something larger than ourselves, something we consider to be divine or of exceptional nobility.* This means we seek to connect to something larger than our immature ego, our little needs. The innate desire for that connection transcends any particular faith or tradition. It does not require a belief in a divinity by any description, nor does it preclude a belief in God or Spirit or the divine. I believe this innate need to be connected to "something larger" exists in all of us, although some may hear that voice more loudly than others. From time to time, our survival needs may trump our awareness of this call. This is why Abraham Maslow identified "self-transcendence" as one of the universal human needs but placed it at the top of his pyramid, indicating that it might only fully emerge when the lower "subsistence" needs are met.

Religion, as I define it, is a specific set of beliefs and practices, usually based on a sacred text, and represented by a community of people. Religions can support people in their spiritual growth, in the fulfillment of that innate need to connect with something greater than themselves, but it is not the only path to spiritual development.

Spiritual Intelligence, as distinct from both spirituality and religion, is a set of skills we develop over time, with practice. It can be developed either within or independent of a religious belief or tradition. The key point to note here, however, is that it does need to be *developed.* I believe we are all born spiritual, but we are not born spiritually intelligent. Spiritual Intelligence takes work and practice. In the same way, a child may be born with musical talent, but unless she learns the skill of playing an instrument, and practices her art consistently she will not grow up to be a great musician.

So what is Spiritual Intelligence? Created with much consideration, my definition of spiritual intelligence is: *The ability to behave with wisdom and compassion, while maintaining inner and outer peace, regardless of the situation.*

This definition grew out of my search for a universal language to describe the goal of human striving. Originally I wanted to use the phrase "behaving with love," because so many of the great traditions talk about love. But "love" in the English language is a very vague and imprecise word. We say, "I love my children," and "I love pizza." I needed something more precise than this, more measurable. One day I came across a definition of love from the East that read: "Love is a bird with two wings. One wing is compassion; the other wing is wisdom. If either wing is broken, the bird cannot fly." I knew as soon as I read those words that I had found what I was looking for. It felt like I was remembering a deep truth that I didn't even know I had forgotten.

Wisdom and compassion became the two pillars of spiritual attainment that I placed at the center of my new definition. I had found the terms that would allow me to "operationalize" this thing called "love." They represent to me the best of the heart and the best of the head coming together to create loving behavior. How can we be loving parents? Loving friends? Leaders? Coworkers? How do we serve the world? We serve the world by being wise and compassionate. We must bring a mature mind and a mature heart to our actions. The word "behave" is also critical in my definition. Spiritual Intelligence must show up in our actions and our behaviors. If we see spiritual development only as an inner experience, if we do not embody it in some exterior, visible way, then I would say we have not yet lived up to the spiritual exemplars we so admire.

The final part of the definition refers to the ability to maintain inner and outer peace, regardless of the situation. I have found that this time-honored spiritual ideal is essential if we are going to act from love. We must hold our wisdom and compassion within a larger container of peacefulness. And the reason I specify "inner and outer" is that a lot of people can fake peacefulness on the outside, yet can be anything but peaceful internally. This is not always a bad thing to do in certain circumstances, but it is a tremendous energy drain. I work with a lot of healthcare providers, and observe them doing a fantastic job of maintaining an appearance of outer peace while interacting with difficult or very upset patients and family members. But I also see the toll this takes over time—the fatigue, stress, and burnout that are endemic in this industry. The kind of peace that is the expression of highly developed Spiritual Intelligence is a peace that comes from the inside. Inner peace generates outer peace without creating fatigue or burnout. Inner peace is therefore more genuine, and less likely to be rattled in times of crisis or stress.

The ability to behave with wisdom and compassion, while maintaining inner and outer peace, regardless of the situation. That is my simple expression of the "ultimate goal" that Maslow was pointing to. I believe it distills the essence of what we find so inspiring and exemplary in those people who are cited, time and time again, as spiritual heroes. And it is a powerful definition, because, as we shall see in this book, it can be broken down into specific "skills" that we can measure, thereby empowering us to take our development into our own hands.

Embracing the Process

All of this talk about ultimate goals and higher potentials may be worrisome to some. You may be wondering: Isn't spirituality about accepting things as they are? What about "being in the moment"? I ask you to consider a paradox. I believe goal-orientation is essential for growth, but that we also reach our goal in every step we take during the process of development. We discover our "optimal state" through the process of development itself—through consciously and freely engaging with our own growth and evolution in the way that only humans seem able to do. In fact, because we are evolving beings, our full flourishing may be a moving target. The destination and the journey are intertwined—one helping to define and redefine the other in a magnificent unfolding.

This is the paradox I ask you to hold as we begin this book. On the one hand, you need to set your sights high enough that it stretches you beyond where you imagine you can go. You need to reach for such a lofty goal that you experience what the mystics have called a "divine discontent," a restlessness and urgency to be the best you can be. On the other hand, you need to trust the process itself and embrace the present moment fully—too much urgency undermines the peacefulness and the wisdom of the process. It can engender harsh self-judgment, which is the opposite of self-compassion, and leads to unproductive and growth-inhibiting relationships with yourself and with others.

Many people feel great urgency these days around personal growth. This is essentially a good thing as the world we are in and the life conditions we are facing require wiser and more compassionate leaders. Indeed, the demands of our planet and our fellow human beings are so desperate that it often seems as if there is simply no time to do the necessary work on ourselves. And yet it is essential that we do our individual work.

Scholars, clinicians, faith practitioners, and philosophers have studied the developmental journey for a long enough time now to have some pretty good pointers to help people "speed up" the process. Yet growing a fuller "self" is like growing a life-sustaining crop of grain. As desperately as we might want it to be done tomorrow, the process can only be accelerated so much. For each of us there is a constraint on how fast we can move and a natural sequence of steps that must be followed. Bestselling business author Stephen Covey calls this "the law of the farm." In order to produce a good crop we must first prepare the ground, plant the seeds, and nurture them. "Quick, easy, free, and fun approaches won't work on the 'farms' of our lives because . . . we're subject to natural laws and governing principles,"[2] he writes. Our challenge is to keep the process as short as possible and yet never be frustrated with the time it is taking or try to skip necessary steps. Trying to move too fast can create the temporary appearance of rapid progress, but big gaps in our development (sometimes known as shadows) will slow us down later. Rushing development is like building on an incomplete foundation, leading to instability and even collapse. Spectacular and tragic falls from grace are too often the result.

So my advice at the beginning of this book and for every day you are alive is this: know that you are perfect just the way you are, *and* that the unfolding of your fullest and highest self is still in front of you. Feel calm and urgent at the same time. Everything is all right—but don't stop working on how it can be better. Don't stop becoming all you can be.

In keeping with this paradox, this book doesn't focus on some static ideal state of "the fully developed human" but on a dynamic process of development. Becom*ing* fully human is not an attainment but a continuous engagement. And the ability to live fully in that engagement is perhaps the most significant spiritual attainment we can aspire to. In my own research, I have found this to be the key to personal growth.

The human self, as I understand it, is by nature not a static entity—it is a *process* of becoming, changing, adapting, contracting, and then expanding. It is affected by external life conditions, such as the culture around it, the physical environment, and the problems it encounters in its struggle to survive and thrive. It is also affected by internal conditions—instinctive habit patterns, emotional and psychological conditioning, and an innate interior drive to become "more" and be more compassionate, wise, and peaceful.

Many of us tend to think of the self as a noun. We refer to ourselves in static terms: I am a human resources manager; I am a mother; I am an American. Try to think of your *self* as a verb, and refer to yourself in dynamic terms. See how it changes your sense of identity and possibility: I am learning and growing; I am considering the pros and cons of the choices in front of me; I am feeling many things at the same time—sad and happy, tired yet excited. Add time parameters to increase the sense of flowing nature of yourself. While I was raised Roman Catholic, I went through a period of agnosticism and now identify myself as a "Zen-Christian" (a Christian influenced by Buddhism and Taoism). Who knows how I will identify myself in ten years.

The Central Question

The "self" is dynamic, flowing, and fascinating. Some people refer to it as the "selfing" to make its dynamic nature more clear. We are flowing all the time, and there are many streams that make up who and what we are. Some aspects of ourselves may be highly developed, while others lag behind. And yet some things remain constant. Some essence of "Cindy" has been here since I was born. As we will discover, the important question is: *Who is in charge of this self-process in all its multi-layered and ever-changing complexity?* Ask yourself: Am I letting the exterior world tell me who I should be, how I should act, and what I should strive for? Or is there a deeper, calmer voice guiding my unfoldment? Am I a bundle of contradictions, seeming to be one person in one moment and another in the next? Or am I doing my best to express integrity and self-consistency as I navigate the complexities of life? Am I feeling aligned with a purpose more universal than the petty and short-term concerns and desires that my ego is feeling today?

Spiritual Intelligence comes down to this essential question: Who is driving your life? Is the calmer, wiser "Higher Self" in charge, or are you driven by an immature, short-sighted ego and/or the beliefs and ideals of others? This central question of who is driving says everything about your capacity to become fully human and the depth of your engagement in the process of growth and development right now.

What we discover, as we pay closer attention to our own choices and actions, is that *we can choose to grow or not.* Who is the "I" that chooses? For much of our lives most of us abdicate the power of this "I that chooses" to our parents, our school, our culture—until for some reason we begin a process of "self-authoring." If you imagine your life as a TV show or a movie, consider that in the first half of your life you are handed a script, a role, and told what you should do and when. With exceptions for teen rebellion we are heavily influenced by this. And even in rebellion, from a certain point of view, we are controlled by the script because we are reacting to the script. We have not yet achieved real freedom of choice. We become self-authoring only when we become aware of which part of our own self is in charge. We then discover that there is in fact a "master system" or observer of the process, sometimes called the Higher Self. This is the part of us that can choose to steer this process of "selfing." Developing the voice of the Higher Self and learning how to follow its guidance is the most vital part of Spiritual Intelligence.

Here is the essence of what Spiritual Intelligence allows us to do: We can mature the ego, gently shift it out of the driver's seat and over into the passenger's seat, and allow our Higher Self to drive the car of our life. That's when the destination suddenly becomes clear, the process speeds up, and we "self" or develop at maximum speed. All the while we are also at peace in the moment, knowing and trusting that the best part of ourselves is in charge, and therefore we are in the best place we could possibly be, right now. As this book illustrates, Spiritual

Intelligence helps us become more conscious of the self-process and the larger world-process in which it is embedded, while gaining mastery over both the self and its relationship with the world.

As we focus on the fuller development of our higher human potential, it is important to keep in mind that the "lower" or less developed aspects of our humanity are not something to be reviled or ashamed of. Being human is a miraculous gift, including our imperfections. But we are like a group of adolescents. We have a tendency to think we know everything but are still quite foolish in many of our ways. Do you laugh at old photos of yourself from middle school or high school? ("Look at those clothes! What were we thinking?") One day we will laugh with compassion at our earlier selves. Right now we need to keep maturing. We need to mature fast enough to prevent unnecessary suffering for ourselves and for many other humans as well as our fellow creatures and the planet we share. We have the amazing capacity, the inner drive, and the interior compass to help us grow up. That is what makes humanity so fascinating and full of potential.

That inner drive is the part of us that instinctively recognizes higher human expression when we see it and that is drawn towards growth and self-actualization. In simple terms, this is what I call the Higher Self. In contrast, the ego, or small self, is the immature, selfish, short-sighted part of us all, the part that wants to things to stay just the way they are. I discuss these different aspects of our human nature in much greater detail later in this book. If you find the terms I use uncomfortable—if they trigger certain reactions or negative patterns for you—don't worry. You will be able to create your own terms. All we need to agree on, at this moment in our journey, is that there are these different drives within each of us—some that are more noble, selfless, and inspired, and others that tend toward pettiness, selfishness, and limitation. If we can acknowledge this simple truth with compassion, we are ready to begin our journey.

T W O

Understanding Intelligences

"As human beings, we have many different ways of representing meaning, many kinds of intelligence."

—Howard Gardner, *Frames of Mind*

Have you ever met anyone who is really smart, but has terrible inter-personal skills? Whenever I ask this question, inevitably people laugh, and say "oh, yes!" Some will volunteer examples—"Sounds like my boss!" or "Have you met my sibling?" After the chuckles die down, however, we get a bit serious. What is going on in cases like this? Indeed, they are very common. How can people be so smart in one area of life and so inept in another? The simple answer is that *there is more than one type of intelligence.* Once we understand this obvious but still surprisingly underappreciated fact, we are more fully able to embrace our own strengths and identify our areas for growth.

In order to focus on the development of Spiritual Intelligence, it is critical to understand how it fits into the matrix of multiple intelligences that make up our humanity. We shall see that Spiritual Intelligence is not just one intelligence among many. When highly developed, it also becomes a source of guidance and direction for the other dimensions of our human potential.

When psychologists first got interested in measuring "intelligence" back in nineteenth-century France, it was generally considered a singular capacity and understood as an ability to reason and solve problems that each human being was born with, to a greater or lesser degree. This capacity was considered difficult to change. The bias of most (though not all) working in this field in the early days was clearly in the direction of "nature over nurture"—the belief that hereditary factors play the major role in determining intelligence and that cultural and environmental factors, including education, are secondary. This belief even gave rise to some unsavory ideas about which humans should be allowed to reproduce so as to optimize the intelligence of society as a whole—a form of social Darwinism. Fortunately, those ideas did not prevail. In our culture we understand that a person's "intelligence" is not simply a matter of genetic inheritance. And increasingly we are seeing that intelligence is not a single "thing."

Not all the early intelligence researchers were social Darwinists. Alfred Binet, father of the modern IQ test, had very different motivations. France had just passed a groundbreaking legislation that was going to require all children to attend school. Such a democratization of education was a radical innovation, and the government knew it would require an expansion of teaching skills to include children who had not been raised in privileged homes. Binet and fellow French psychologist Théodore Simon developed the Binet-Simon test to provide teachers with a fair and objective way to assess which children would require more of their time and attention. Unfortunately others seized on his test as a tool for much less positive forms of discrimination, including the early-twentieth-century eugenics movement in the United States.

The field of IQ remains controversial to this day. Many people feel mistreated by standard IQ testing. In very young students it is now known that mood, health, and any form of social anxiety can impair scores on task-based IQ assessments. Even among older students, some are simply poor test-takers. Perhaps you or a sibling or friend have dealt with some form of learning disability such as dyslexia. If so, you know that conditions like this do not necessarily indicate a lack of intelligence, but rather a difficulty in processing certain kinds of information. However, students with learning disabilities are often considered "less intelligent" by those unaware of the nuances of this field.

We now know that human beings are complex mixtures of talents and skills. People with high functioning autism, or Asperger's syndrome, can be brilliant at some tasks yet interpersonally clumsy. An example many of us will remember is Dustin Hoffman's character Raymond in the movie *Rain Man.* He could compute enormous numbers in his head but did not understand the basics of interpersonal communication. Individuals who fail every test in school sometimes turn out to be creative or athletic geniuses. A child who seems low in conventional IQ may turn out to be socially gifted, like a little girl who can describe to you the web of friendships among all thirty children in her classroom. She notices who eats lunch together and who is sad or happy on a given day. Examples like these and many more make it clear that there is more to intelligence than the narrow range of abilities that are measured by conventional psychometric testing.

Given this, it is hardly surprising that even among those who cling to the idea of a singular "general" intelligence, no standard definition of the term has yet been agreed upon. Artificial Intelligence researchers S. Legg and M. Hutter have collected as many as seventy varying definitions from credible dictionaries and psychologists,[3] proving American psychologist and psychometrician Robert J. Sternberg's remark that "Viewed narrowly, there seem to be almost as many definitions of intelligence as there were experts asked to define it."[4]

Sternberg was one of the first to challenge the traditional psychometric "it's one thing" approach to intelligence. He proposed a "triarchic" view of intelligence that divides it into three parts: Analytic, Creative, and Practical. Psychologist Howard Gardner went even further in his breakthrough 1983 book *Frames of Mind,* proposing that human beings possess multiple intelligences in addition to what is commonly measured on an IQ test. "Human beings are better thought of as possessing a number of relatively independent faculties," he writes, "rather than as having a certain amount of intellectual horsepower (or IQ) that can be simply channeled in one or another direction. I decided to search for a better formulation of human intelligence. I proposed a new definition: *an intelligence is a psychobiological potential to process information so as to solve problems or to fashion products that are valued in at least one cultural context.*"[5]

It's not the most elegant or easy-to-remember definition, but it gave Gardner a set of criteria by which to identify seven distinct intelligences. Based on his empirical work with both normal and gifted children and also with brain-damaged patients, his book discussed seven types of intelligence:

1. Linguistic (spoken and written language—comprehending and composing)
2. Logical-mathematical
3. Musical (performance, composition, appreciation)
4. Bodily-kinesthetic (physical strength and coordination—important for professional athletes or dancers, skilled surgeons, some craftspeople)
5. Spatial (recognizing patterns of space—important for pilots, navigators, sculptors, architects)
6. Interpersonal (understanding intentions, motivations, and desires of others)
7. Intrapersonal (understanding one's own desires, fears, and capacities, and using this information to manage your own life)

In more recent writings Gardner added an eighth—naturalist intelligence—and continues to speculate about a possible ninth—existential intelligence.

This may all seem like a very complex way of approaching the notion of intelligence. It can be a fascinating lens through which to begin to explain many of the things we all encounter as we grow up and navigate school, career choices, and relationships. It can help us to understand why we may have preferences for certain types of activities or why some skills come easily to us while others seem to go against the grain. But what is the *practical* value of knowing what an intelligence is, and how many different ones we possess? What is the average person, who is not interested in arguing over fancy nuances and long definitions, to do with this concept of multiple intelligences? If we understand the concept *just well enough* we can use it to optimize our own lives. We need to explore these questions: What are my gifts? What can I change? What can't I change? And, the bottom line: If I want to get better at something, *how* can I do that?

With this kind of pragmatic application foremost in my mind, I have created my own definition of intelligence that synthesizes and attempts to simplify some of the many definitions already out there. Intelligence is made up of three parts: nature, nurture, and results. Therefore, intelligence is:

Your innate potential (nature) that is:

- brought into form through practice (nurture/effort) AND

- results in adeptness or appropriately reasoned behavior or choice.

To illustrate this definition, let's take the example of musical intelligence. Imagine that a child is born musically gifted (nature). Through some fortunate accident of genetics, she has the innate potential to be a world-class pianist. But she is born into a family with little appreciation of music in circumstances where the very idea of taking music lessons would seem like a ridiculous luxury as her parents struggle to put food on the table. She is never exposed to a piano, never studies music theory, never practices her art, and therefore does not develop her musical potential. Now imagine that the same child is born into very different circumstances. She has the same gift of nature, but in this instance her family appreciates and encourages music, giving her the opportunity to bring potential into form through practice (nurture). In this case, the end result will be musical intelligence—an ability to inspire others and herself with the beauty of original compositions played with precision and passion.

The highest potentials of particular intelligences, like unusual mathematical capacity or physical agility, may be decided for us before we leave our mother's womb. People with the innate capacity to become physicists at the level of Albert Einstein or Stephen Hawking are rare. Yet even the gifted must study and learn their crafts. Athletes must train their bodies into finely tuned vehicles if their natural gifts of strength, agility, or speed are to flourish. And yet training alone is not enough. You or I could perform the exact same workout routines as Michael Jordan or another amazing athlete every day, but we would not be able to match his physical intelligence.

Examples like these, involving unusual gifts and potentials, are helpful for understanding how nature and nurture combine to create a particular intelligence. Most of us, however, are less concerned about whether we will fulfill some innate potential to become the next Einstein and more concerned about how we can become more effective, productive, and happy in our work and our relationships. Unless you long to be a pilot or an architect, spatial intelligence may not be high on your list of concerns. Unless you cherish dreams of playing Carnegie Hall, musical intelligence may not be something you give a lot of thought to. But I am sure you do give thought to concerns like: How can I take better care of myself so I get sick less often? How can I learn to think more clearly and rationally about the pros and cons of my decisions? How can I improve my relationship with my spouse, my boss, or my team? How can I make wiser choices and be more awake to the potential impact of my actions on others?

Questions like these, which trouble most of us at different points in our lives, relate to what I have identified as the four key intelligences that are essential for living a successful, happy, and meaningful life. Theorists like Gardner can sit and ponder over whether there are seven or eight or nine intelligences, but for most of us four are plenty to be worrying about. The key intelligences are: Physical Intelligence (PQ), Cognitive Intelligence (IQ), Emotional Intelligence (EQ), and Spiritual Intelligence (SQ). This book focuses on the last, and least understood, of the four: Spiritual Intelligence. But before we venture into that less-charted terrain, it is essential to have a basic grasp of the other three key intelligences and to understand how all four work together.

These four intelligences are relevant to all human beings. With the exception of those who suffer from rare disorders, we are all born with the basic "wiring" for each of these intelligences. For example, as far as Emotional Intelligence is concerned, most of us are born with the emotional circuitry already in place. In the natural course of events we develop emotional *reactions*. However, nature does not take care of everything. We have to make an effort to nurture our emotional intelligence through learning the skills to manage those reactions in a responsible, effective way. We are born with the "wiring" for emotions, but we are not born emotionally intelligent. Emotional intelligence, however, is clearly learnable, unless one suffers from a serious psychobiological disorder. I have found the same to be true of SQ. We know this because interventions to teach/coach EQ and SQ skills to individuals have been proven to work, and because both intelligences are strongly correlated with age, meaning these intelligences tend to increase as the person grows older. But once again, there is nothing *guaranteed* about EQ or SQ skill development. Not *everyone* gets better at these skills with age. Have you met people in their sixties or beyond who *still* don't have good interpersonal skills? I suspect you have. This is because it takes willingness, effort, and sometimes mentoring to learn these skills. Most people have a capacity to learn these skills—a capacity that increases with age—but it's not automatic. The good news is that we can nurture ourselves to develop these skills and achieve the results we care about.

As you begin to consider these four intelligences and to engage with your own development, it is important to remember that there is no fixed or preestablished amount of any intelligence that you "must" have. Physical, Cognitive, Emotional, and Spiritual Intelligences need to be developed to the level necessary to meet the demands of *your* life and fulfill your desire to grow. The degree to which you might choose to focus on and develop a particular intelligence depends on the role(s) you want to fill and the results you want to achieve. Want to be a parent or care for young children? You will need a lot of patience and emotional self-management skills—and physical stamina. Want to pilot a space flight? Better be willing to put in long hours in the science fields (IQ), develop outstanding teamwork (EQ and SQ), and be in top physical condition (PQ). Want to run a Fortune 500 company? You had better have the stamina of a corporate athlete, be able to fly through time zones, deal with jet lag and not enough sleep, and combine that with the high IQ, EQ and—yes—SQ that will be required for you to succeed.

Finally, these intelligences have interesting relationships to each other. You can think of them as being both independent and interconnected. The independent model looks like Figure 2.1:

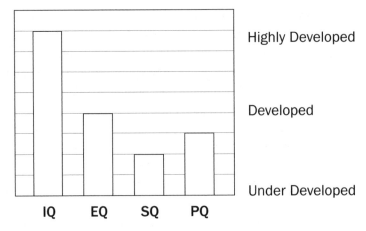

Highly Developed

Developed

Under Developed

IQ   EQ   SQ   PQ

Figure 2.1 The Parallel Lines Model

In this model, the lines of intelligence grow fairly independently. You can be highly developed in one or two intelligences, and underdeveloped or average development in the others.

The simplest interconnected model can be represented as a pyramid, similar to Maslow's Hierarchy of Needs.

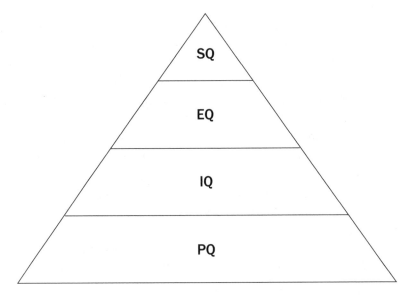

Figure 2.2 The Pyramid Model

Physical Intelligence (PQ)

The base of the pyramid—our PQ—needs to be strong in order to support the "weight" of the levels above. While many people take it for granted, PQ is foundational. When we don't take care of our bodies everything else suffers. I define PQ simply as "body awareness and skillful use."

You can think of the pyramid model (Figure 2.2) as an oversimplified representation of the developmental sequence by which these intelligences emerge. PQ comes earliest in the life cycle, as we struggle to master the physical body. I watched our baby grandson learning to roll over and now he is trying to crawl. What an awesome amount of work it takes to learn how to control our human bodies! PQ is the first of the four intelligences that we have to devote serious time to developing, but it is also interesting to note that it becomes an important focus later in life as well. As we pass midlife, being physically intelligent means remembering to take proper care of our bodies—from nutrition, exercise, and sleep to preventative medical care. At this later point in life you can *feel* the foundational nature of PQ in ways that you may not be so conscious of in your carefree teens or twenties.

If PQ is not sufficiently developed and maintained, any attempts to develop all the other intelligences will be stunted. As Maslow demonstrated in his Hierarchy of Needs, the lower-level ("deficiency") needs generally must be fulfilled before the individual can become concerned about some of the higher level (being) needs. "A hungry man may willingly surrender his need for self-respect in order to stay alive; but once he can feed, shelter, and clothe himself, he becomes likely to seek higher needs."[6] The same applies when we look at human development through the lens of multiple intelligences. If your physical intelligence is underdeveloped, you will not have the focus or energy to develop or use cognitive, emotional, or spiritual skills. When we are exhausted, or if our hormones are out of balance or our blood sugar levels too low, even those with high IQ, EQ, and SQ are likely to make mistakes in logic, become inconsiderate, and see things from a narrow self-interested point of view. However, if your physical body is in good order and getting the support it needs to function optimally, your attention is freed up for other kinds of intelligence; just as in childhood, once we have mastered the basic physical skill of walking we can begin to develop our other intelligences, beginning with IQ.

Cognitive Intelligence (IQ)

By the time the developing child is ready to go to school, his focus has shifted to IQ development. This is not to say that IQ, or cognitive intelligence, was not developing beforehand or that PQ stops developing. But the primary focus shifts as the child learns logical thinking, language skills, and other basics he needs to function in a complex industrialized society. IQ is the kind of intelligence we are most familiar with and its development is supported by our education systems. Initially, this kind of development is focused on mathematical and linguistic capacities and basic technical skills. In later life, this intelligence continues to develop and includes the important attainment of higher levels of cognitive complexity, such as the ability to consider many perspectives simultaneously. For example, in a business setting it is this capacity that allows a highly conscious leader to consider the impact of her decisions on all stakeholders, as well as on the cultural, economic, and other systems in which she and her business are embedded. In psychology this is sometimes referred to as the ability to think "systemically" and "meta-systemically." Developing this higher level of cognitive complexity seems to be tied to the development of EQ and SQ.

Emotional Intelligence

By the time we leave school, we move into the domain of significant behavioral emotional intelligence development. Again, EQ has been developing all along, but now our physical brain has actually changed. Scientists have discovered that the human brain doesn't finish developing until somewhere between the ages of 22 and 25. And full EQ capacity is dependent on the final surge of development in the prefrontal lobes of the neocortex. This begins around the age of 11 and completes between the ages of 22 and 25. Our prefrontal cortex acts as the "executive decision making center" of the brain, and allows us to use our higher-brain activities to "trump" our lower impulses and fears that are activated from the older parts of the brain. This explains why our college years, or early years in the workplace, are the key time of life for the development of EQ skills. It's a good thing that that prefrontal cortex "comes online" during these years, because life gets much more complex as we move away from home, start a family and/or a career, and find ourselves needing to negotiate complex relationships in both domains.

Emotional intelligence has been defined in numerous ways, but essentially it relates to our interpersonal skills, founded on emotional self-awareness and empathy and emotional self-management. In my own work I have adopted the most well-used and field-tested model of EQ, developed by Daniel Goleman and Richard Boyatzis. However, I learned about EQ the hard way, long before I had heard of Goleman's work or even knew the term.

After starting my first job, I found out pretty quickly that being "book-smart," or having a high IQ, is not necessarily the only ingredient to being successful. When I graduated from Duke University (a school that prides itself on being intellectually demanding) and began my career, I was, as my supervisors gently pointed out to me, very smart and very annoying. "You're a hard worker, you're really bright, but you need to work on your interpersonal skills. You're coming across as arrogant and pushy," was the essence of what I was told, gently but firmly. Today we would call what I was lacking "emotional intelligence." I had plenty of IQ but not enough EQ. I was hammering people with my IQ and not getting the results I desired. So I stumbled my way into the world of more advanced interpersonal skills, beginning with emotional self-awareness.

The story of my rather awkward start at naming my own emotions is both funny and instructive. Due to upheaval in my personal life, I'd started therapy at around the same time as I was getting the constructive feedback at work regarding my interpersonal skills. Each week I would talk with my therapist about something that was going on, and he would ask, "How do you feel about that?" At the time I thought this an odd question to ask, and I'd answer, "Well, I think X." He would smile patiently and point out, "I didn't ask you what you *thought*. I asked you what you *felt*." "I don't really have any feelings about that," I'd say. He would smile again. We would end the session and begin again the next week.

You might laugh, but I have found a great many people who are just as clueless now as I was then about detecting and naming emotions. I grew up as a fan of the original Star Trek series. I adored Mr. Spock. I thought the Vulcans had it all figured out. Logic would make the world a peaceful place. So I developed my IQ and my "thinking" skills and didn't put effort into "feeling skills." I learned how to be polite and respectful, as defined by my parents, but I suppressed my own emotions to the point where I literally had no awareness of them.

Not being one who likes to fail tests, however, I soon figured I should do some homework before seeing my therapist again. I created a spreadsheet of "emotion words," alphabetizing them for quick and easy reference. You may think I'm joking, but I'm not. Before each week's therapy session, I would think about the events of the week and try to match them to words on the list, putting names on my emotions. Eventually I got to the point where I could say, "This situation made me angry" or "that event made me sad." As I got better and better at it, I became able, though not without effort, to name an emotion within minutes after an event occurred. I had to pause, clear my mind, and search for the best name for the feeling I had in reaction to what just happened. It was as if I were tearing down a wall around my emotions, brick by brick. It was such a proud day when my therapist and I realized the time gap between the event or interaction and the identification of the feeling was narrowing. He joked that "one day we'll get you to real-time emotions." Sure enough, one day it happened. There was a feeling like a "pop!" inside my head. The last brick fell. I could name my emotions as they were arising and I could see what was triggering them.

The activation and development of this new "emotional muscle" gave me so much power to love myself and develop myself. One of the first gifts that resulted from my newfound self-awareness was the development of empathy. It was embarrassing to see how I had been creating negative emotions in others with my previous behaviors. Eventually, through empathy and interior work, a well-calibrated set of communication skills was born. For example, I was able to "self-manage" better, not reacting too loudly or withdrawing when upset. I learned how to influence others, to develop and mentor and be a good teammate.

At the same time that I was undergoing my "EQ awakening," Daniel Goleman and many others, unbeknownst to me, were researching the same developmental journey I was on and showing its crucial importance for personal and professional leadership. In 1995 Goleman popularized the term "emotional intelligence" in his book of the same name, and later he introduced it to the world of business in his 1998 *Harvard Business Review* article. While dismissed by some in the research community as "pop science," the model of EQ created by Daniel Goleman and Richard Boyatzis has become the most widely used approach to EQ in the business world. Backing up his ideas (which were unconventional in business at the time) with solid research at nearly 200 global companies, Goleman was able to tell "a persuasive story about the link between a company's success and the emotional intelligence of its leaders" and to demonstrate that "people can, if they take the right approach, develop their emotional intelligence."[7]

Thanks to Goleman's work, EQ soon entered the common parlance. In fact, Goleman himself wryly pointed out in his introduction to the tenth anniversary edition of his bestseller that emotional intelligence as a concept had found its way into cartoon strips like *Dilbert,* as well as "lovelorn personal ads" and even a shampoo bottle. While the scientific mainstream may still debate the notion of multiple intelligences, popular culture has indeed embraced it with a vengeance. It seems like every other week a new "intelligence" is coined—on a single shelf in my local bookstore I found titles on business intelligence, practical intelligence, relational intelligence, social intelligence, and financial intelligence. I even recently received an invitation to a workshop on "theatrical intelligence," with the tagline: "Discover the role you were born to play."

For all the popularity of the idea, however, it is interesting how limited views of intelligence still persist. *New York Times* columnist David Brooks highlighted these phenomena recently in an insightful piece responding to the national furor that occurred around the publication of Amy Chua's 2011 book *Battle Hymn of the Tiger Mother.* The Chinese immigrant author proudly describes how she raised her two daughters, which included forbidding play dates, sleepovers, TV, and video games, and insisting they exhaustively practice their musical instruments and study. Not surprisingly, Chua's daughters are straight-A students and prize-winning musicians. But Americans have been incensed at her harsh and authoritarian tactics.

In his thoughtful column, Brooks writes: "I have the opposite problem with Chua. I believe she's coddling her children. She's protecting them from the most intellectually demanding activities because she doesn't understand what's cognitively difficult and what isn't." He goes on to explain that, "practicing a piece of music for four hours requires focused attention, but it is nowhere near as cognitively demanding as a sleepover with 14-year-old girls. Managing status rivalries, negotiating group dynamics, understanding social norms, navigating the distinction between self and group—these and other social tests impose cognitive demands that blow away any intense tutoring session or a class at Yale."[8]

While he does not explicitly use the term, what Brooks is pointing to is the difference and the synergy between IQ and EQ. Brooks is right when he concludes that, "in some important ways the school cafeteria is more intellectually demanding than the library." In other words, EQ is a separate and very demanding set of skills that are required to negotiate the world of other humans. And developing these skills fosters rather than impedes our cognitive growth.

The diagram on page 29 illustrates the eighteen skills of emotional intelligence as described by Daniel Goleman and Richard Boyatzis. Goleman highlights three skills as especially important foundations for building relationship skills (boldface in the diagram): emotional self-awareness, empathy, and emotional self-control.

Emotional self-awareness is the skill I taught myself using my list of "feeling words": the ability to name our own emotions accurately and to understand what triggered them. It is a crucial skill because if we do not understand our own emotions it is nearly impossible to accurately understand and have empathy with another person's emotions. Furthermore, if we do not understand our own emotions and what triggers them, it is hard to exercise appropriate self-control. Empathy (the ability to emotionally put ourselves in the shoes of another) and emotional self-control (the ability to make appropriate choices in the face of strong emotions) are essential if we are to be effective in relating to other human beings. These skills matter in our personal lives and in our professional ones. If we cannot "feel with" others, we cannot accurately predict the emotional reactions our coworkers, our employees, our customers, or our shareholders might have in response to decisions we make. We will fail to factor in relevant data.

"Emotional Competency Framework"

SELF-AWARENESS

- Emotional Self-Awareness
- Accurate Self-Assessment
- Self-Confidence

SOCIAL AWARENESS

- Empathy
- Organizational Awareness
- Service Orientation

SELF-MANAGEMENT

- Emotional Self-Control
- Transparency
- Adaptability
- Achievement Orientation
- Initiative
- Optimism

SOCIAL SKILLS

- Developing Others
- Inspirational Leadership
- Influence
- Change Catalyst
- Conflict Management
- Teamwork & Collaboration

Figure 2.3 The "Four Quadrants and Eighteen Skills of Emotional Intelligence" Framework Developed by Daniel Goleman and Richard Boyatzis.

The media is filled with the spectacular falls from grace of CEOs like Rupert Murdoch, who were clueless about how they would be perceived by others. Furthermore, emotional self-awareness and empathy are foundational as we begin our work with Spiritual Intelligence. And SQ development, once begun, can accelerate our IQ development in the realm of cognitive complexity, our EQ growth as well as our ability to maintain a healthy PQ. SQ forms a virtuous developmental circle with these other intelligences.

Spiritual Intelligence

The notion of SQ is less accepted and even harder to pin down than EQ, but it is slowly becoming more mainstream in scientific inquiry and in business and philosophical/psychological discussion. Spiritual intelligence has been identified as a key component of leadership by author Stephen Covey. Many people attribute the term to Danah Zohar, who introduced the idea in her book *ReWiring the Corporate Brain,* and developed it, with Ian Marshall, in subsequent books, including *SQ: The Ultimate Intelligence.* Unfortunately, Zohar and Marshall defined SQ as something that "cannot be quantified,"[9] making their approach limited in its usefulness as a path for personal growth or as a tool for research or for leadership development.

As explained in the previous chapter, I define SQ as "the ability to behave with wisdom and compassion, while maintaining inner and outer peace, regardless of the circumstances." Developmentally, SQ tends to come last among the four key intelligences. In my own development and my work with others, I have found that this is because it depends upon some EQ development preceding it—particularly the skills of emotional self-awareness and empathy. Without some self-awareness and reflective capacity, the interior work of SQ cannot proceed. And without empathy, compassion (which is a higher level skill than empathy) cannot be developed. Interestingly, most people experience, as I have, that once they begin their SQ work it acts to accelerate and amplify their EQ skill development, forming a virtuous and reinforcing circle. A little EQ enables SQ to start, which amplifies and nourishes more EQ development, which in turn feeds into more SQ development.

Howard Gardner chose not to include spiritual intelligence amongst his intelligences due to the challenge of codifying quantifiable scientific criteria.[10] Later, Gardner suggested an "existential intelligence" as viable,[11] which subsequent researchers have attempted to connect with spirituality. Gardner himself, however, remains cautious. "It seems more responsible to carve out that area of spirituality closest 'in spirit' to the other intelligences and then . . . ascertain how this candidate intelligence fares. In doing so, I think it best to put aside the term spiritual, with its manifest and problematic connotations, and to speak instead of an intelligence that explores the nature of existence in its multifarious guises. Thus, an explicit concern with spiritual or religious matters would be one variety—often the most important variety—of an existential intelligence."

Gardner's caution is understandable. Religion and spirituality can be a touchy subject full of vague definitions and lots of emotion. Many suggest that anything connected to spiritual skills cannot be measured by traditional means, while others maintain that, like most constructs related to how we think and behave, some degree of measurement is possible. I believe it is not only possible, but essential, to measure SQ. Rather than limiting it to a particular subset of our broader existential concerns, I have come to understand SQ as playing a foundational role in all of our intelligences. I see it as an *integrating intelligence*—a "capstone" that links and amplifies our rational and emotional capacities. As we discussed in the previous chapter, it is SQ that helps us become more conscious of "who is driving the car," enabling us to take greater ownership of our own growth in all its many dimensions. For this reason, I would concur with author Stephen Covey that, "Spiritual intelligence is the central and most fundamental of all the intelligences, because it becomes the source of guidance for the other[s]."[12]

THREE

Measuring the Immeasurable

*"An experiment is a question
which science poses to Nature,
and a measurement is the recording
of Nature's answer."*

—Max Planck
Scientific Autobiography (1949)

W|hen it comes to matters of the spirit, many people consider them to be immeasurable by nature. So, given that this book explores a model that looks at spiritual intelligence as a "skill-set," and I refer continually to the results of the instrument that I have created to measure these skills, it seems important to take a moment to discuss the delicate, challenging, controversial, and I believe necessary and rewarding task of measuring matters of the spirit.

Spiritual growth, as anyone who has even momentarily set foot on that time-honored road will know, is one of life's most rewarding and most frustrating endeavors. So many different paths seem to guarantee solutions. So many spiritual teachers who initially seem to have the answers turn out to have profound personal blind spots. We search for answers outside ourselves—from spiritual authorities, from sacred scriptures, from whatever we think of as God or the Divine—but we don't know how to do the work fully on the inside. The hunger and restlessness that draws us to the spiritual path is one of the most precious sentiments that human beings experience because it is our doorway to growth. But too often, after some time on the path, we are dulled by cynicism, confusion, or frustration, and we lose touch with this delicate longing.

It was this predicament that inspired me to create the Spiritual Intelligence Assessment (SQ21) in the hope and sincere intention that it might be a step in a more helpful direction. I do not claim that this is the ultimate and final answer to how we develop our spiritual skills. But I do believe it's an important step forward in empowering individuals to take more responsibility for their own spiritual growth. It helps us think critically about what works and what doesn't work. And there is no incompatibility between spirituality and critical thinking.

We need tools to help us more accurately observe and analyze. Which brings us to the matter of measurement, and the possibility of a more systematic approach to finding out what makes us more spiritually intelligent. Almost all of the great saints, sages, and seers of the past have maintained, as philosopher Ken Wilber points out, that "Spirit," by whatever name, "is actually ineffable, unspeakable, utterly beyond words, symbols and logic."[13] I agree with this description. When we are talking about the source of life—whether you would call that the Ground of Being, God, the Tao, the Cosmos, or something else—we are speaking of something that is beyond words and concepts. Meditators and spiritual practitioners across the world report finding a place of pure non-duality or transcendent oneness wherein there is no longer even an observer self. In this state there are no words or concepts—there is only what IS. Words seem to be inappropriate constraints on this experience—somehow too crude, too harsh, too limited. To measure this "ground of being" would be like applying a childhood ability to count blocks to a problem of quantum physics—a complete disconnect.

I want to assure you that the SQ21 does not attempt to quantify or measure Spirit in this sense. It does, however, ask if you have ever had an experience of transcendent oneness. But it is up to you to define what "transcendent oneness" means. In a sense, you are the only one who can. So while I would never undertake the impossible task of "measuring Spirit," I have undertaken the realistic task of helping you to self-assess, as one skill among twenty-one, your experience of connection with transcendent oneness.

As I pointed out in the opening chapter of this book, I also make a distinction between spirituality and Spiritual Intelligence. I define "spirituality" as the innate human need to be connected to something larger than ourselves, something we consider to be divine or of exceptional nobility. I see spirituality as an innate motivator—a high-level human need, as Maslow showed at the top of his pyramid—that emerges in consciousness when the conditions are right. Spiritual Intelligence is a set of skills we develop over time, with practice. When I speak about measurement, I'm speaking about measuring those specific SQ skills.

One final clarification: When I talk about measuring SQ, I am not referring to biological measures, such as the tracking of brain-wave patterns while you meditate, or the study of particular hormones released during a moment of connection with the divine. Although neuroscience's contributions to the study of experiences of Spirit, our innate spirituality, and our Spiritual Intelligence are fascinating, the SQ21 is not a biological measure. I do pay attention to those studies, and what I can tell you is that neuroscience does support the ideas I propose. For example, in emotional intelligence we know that there are two key parts of the brain involved: the limbic system (which includes our fight or flight systems) and the neocortex. As we gain in emotional intelligence we begin to manage the limbic system better through using our neocortex—especially the prefrontal cortex—the part of the brain that is created around age 11 and becomes fully "wired" by the age of about 22 to 25 years. SQ demands even more neocortex-limbic integration and guidance from our highest brain functions. It demands that we go beyond managing our reactions. We actually start to change how we react with conscious intention and practice. Purely scientific approaches, however, can go too far, become intent on removing all the mystery and the miracles from the spiritual dimension of life. I do not want to err on the side of this materialistic fallacy, nor do I want to buy into the notion that nothing "spiritual" can be measured.

I am a great believer in the power of measurement because I believe in development. Spiritual Intelligence, as previously discussed, is not something we're born with. It needs to be developed, and if we want to develop it, we need to have some sense of what the goal is. If you were to get into your car and pull out of the driveway with no sense of where you were going, that would make no sense. To run your life that way makes even less sense. As the Roman philosopher Seneca said, "If you do not know what harbor you sail for, no wind is favorable."[14]

I was a girl scout. I am now a businessperson. What both domains have taught me is that it is essential to plan where we are going and what we will need to get there, and then execute the plan, allowing for unexpected difficulties and surprising new opportunities. Why would we treat our own lives, and our spiritual growth, specifically, as less important? Do we take enough time to consider where we have come from, where we are now, and what our ultimate goal is?

The Power of Measurement

"If you can't measure it you can't manage it," I often tell my clients, and this doesn't just apply in business. Those of us who strive to be self-authoring, self-actualizing drivers of our own development need to be able to "manage" the business of our own growth. This is not to disagree with those who caution that some spiritual matters are immeasurable. These are a pair of simultaneous truths. If we cannot describe the goal or steward ourselves in some way toward the goal, it's very difficult to make progress This implies the need to define what skills we are trying to develop in our pursuit of personal growth and assess our progress. Simultaneously we need to hold these measures as "always partial" and remain humble in the face of the somewhat mysterious processes of human development.

Assessing spiritual intelligence may sound like an overly mechanical approach. But that is not a sufficient reason to abandon the effort to create the best assessment we can—and then continue to improve on it. I prefer an open-minded approach: hypothesis and testing. My hypothesis: finding a way to define, assess, and develop spiritual skills is both possible and useful. So far, a great many clients would agree.

The idea for the SQ21 began to germinate when I worked at Exxon, as I pondered the fact that my own spiritual work was having such a positive impact on my own productivity and effectiveness and on those I was working with. It was frustrating to me that within the human resources culture, I really couldn't tell people about the "secret sauce" that was making me so effective. Later when the book Emotional Intelligence was published, I knew there was now a precedent for what I needed to do. I became certified in the Daniel Goleman/Richard Boyatzis methodology, and attended a large EQ conference with Daniel Goleman, Richard Boyatzis, and many other key researchers. As I listened to the various presentations, appreciating the rationality and the rigor that was being brought to the topic, I thought, somebody needs to do for Spiritual Intelligence what Boyatzis and Goleman have done for Emotional Intelligence.

I quit Exxon in 2000 to seek out the researchers who were doing this work. I couldn't find them. The theology schools were studying measures of religiosity. Psychology seems to like studying optimism, resilience, and stress management but, especially then, wanted to stay away from spirituality. Business schools weren't doing it and big consulting companies seemed scared of it. So since nobody was doing it, I finally nominated myself. I looked in the mirror one day and asked myself, "Do you really want to do this?" And I answered with a firm "Yes," and a reassurance: "Hey, no one knows who you are anyway. What have you got to lose?"

Creating the SQ21 Assessment Tool

Since that decision to create an assessment, a lot of hard work and hundreds of thousands of dollars have gone into the creation and validation of this self-assessment.[15] The basic process I used to create it was to ask myself the same questions discussed earlier in the book, and many more, including: Who are the spiritual leaders people admire? What are the traits people admire? How do those traits show up as behaviors and skills?

At the beginning, I set out some hypotheses: If these are in fact skills, I should be able to describe a skill from a low level (novice) to a high level (expert). The expert-level skills should sound like the skills that would create these spiritual leaders. These skills should be describable in a faith-neutral and faith-friendly way. This SQ model should not conflict with scientific understanding. The skills should be teachable.

I also started with another important hypothesis: that SQ skills would fall into four quadrants that would reflect a "step up" from the EQ skills of Goleman/Boyatzis.[16] So I began by drawing four boxes and seeing what fell into them. The map I eventually came to is shown in Figure 3.1 below, beside the EQ quadrants.

As with Goleman/Boyatzis, who see their lower right quadrant of Social Skills as the outcome of the other three boxes, I saw the box I called Social Mastery and Spiritual Presence as the outcome of developing skills in the other three quadrants.

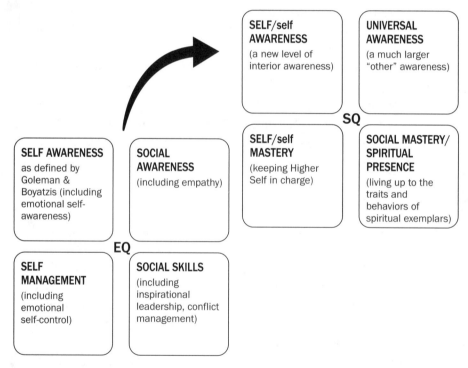

Figure 3.1 Relationship between EQ and SQ

From this beginning I populated the boxes by examining the skills that spiritual exemplars demonstrated as a group. I slowly evolved twenty-one skills, each described from level 1 to level 5 (novice to mastery levels). I created a questionnaire to assess each skill, and hired Customer Value

Systems, a Houston-based consulting firm with deep expertise in survey creation and statistics, to be sure I had created questions for each level of each skill in ways that were clear and scorable (usually on a Likert scale), and that the whole assessment process met PhD-levels of rigor. I formed "focus groups" with clients that were facilitated by Customer Value Systems. In these sessions we asked participants including nurses, hospital chaplains trained in interfaith situations, and people in a variety of administrative jobs to help clarify words, synonyms, and concepts in a way that would work for people of many faiths and be acceptable in the diversity-sensitive world of the workplace. With the help of my friend Dr. Judith Neal,[17] I then created a subject-matter expert group of coaches and consultants working in the nascent field of "spirituality in the workplace." This group of people agreed to be our "alpha pilot" group. They took the assessment, one quadrant at a time, and gave me feedback in a very detailed way about the order of the levels and the clarity of the language and the scoring and reporting process. This group of practitioners understood my goal of attempting to be faith-friendly and faith-neutral and to get over the hurdles of scientific/psychometric respectability. They understood what I was attempting to do for Spiritual Intelligence and instinctively knew the value of these skills in work and in life from their own personal and professional experience.

We updated the four-quadrant version of the SQ21, based on all the valuable input received, and ran a beta pilot. Over five hundred people participated, and we got extremely high internal reliability scores with good comments from participants. "Just taking this survey was useful," one woman told me. "It made me think about things I haven't thought about in years." A few offered ideas for improvement. We tweaked again.

In 2004 I presented the SQ model to participants at the World Business Academy conference in Santa Barbara, California. Deepak Chopra was in the audience and commented that the assessment "seems to be very complete—covering all the yogas." We asked participants at the conference to take the SQ21 and give us their feedback, and over 100 did so. Since these were all businesspeople—visionaries but living in the real world of bottom-line impacts—I considered it a really important test of the concepts, the wording of the questions, and report quality. Feedback was very positive. A few minor tweaks were suggested and implemented. Then we "locked down" on SQ21 version 1.0—the first commercially available version.

The resulting SQ21 self-assessment was—and still is—an online instrument that asks approximately 170 questions to measure the twenty-one skills. Each skill has a skill development score from zero (have not yet begun development) to five (highest level measured), and in the report that people receive once they have taken the test, they are told their skill development level based on the answers given. This is given as both a numeric result (zero to 5) and as a paragraph of description of what that skill level looks like behaviorally. Everyone receives a suggested "next step" for every skill. Even a person who scores a 5 (max) on skill development receives a suggested "next step" to continue growing or sustaining that level of development.

Additional research since 2004 has included construct validation and cross-correlation with an assessment measuring stages of adult development. (For more detail on these research projects and on the overall process of creating and validating the SQ21, please see the Appendix.) Research continues. Improving the SQ21, and the whole domain of Spiritual Intelligence, will be and should be an ongoing process.

"The Most Precious Zero"

When it comes to actually scoring the self-assessment, a lot of emotional buttons can get pushed. Even those who are enthusiastic about the idea of measurement sometimes start to feel different if they start to see scores with numbers that are low. It's important to remember that the reason we are measuring is not to judge ourselves or one another, but to allow ourselves to grow, develop, and become more fully who we are. If you don't know where you are, how can you know what next steps you can take to move forward in your development?

The following is a wonderful story that illustrates just how important this is. A woman named Jane, a Unity Church member, participated in one of the programs I co-developed with the Unity leadership. As part of the program, she took the SQ21. "It really got my attention in a way I would not have expected," she told me afterwards. Under the heading "Commitment to Spiritual Growth," she had scored a zero. "I was shocked," she admitted. "Good grades and test scores have always been important to me."

The report included some explanation of what her score could mean, and suggestions for next steps. There are two questions that can create a zero on this skill. One is related to the belief system in which you were raised. This was the question that had led to Jane's zero. Based on this fact, I suggested that she would benefit by finding some forgiveness and healing with her past, and that she consider contacting people from the church of her childhood—a spiritual community that she had rejected, feeling that it was judgmental and intolerant of alternative spiritual paths. "This was the last thing I wanted to do," she confessed. "However, a wiser part of me was opening up, so I let Spirit know that I was willing—just not all that excited about it."

Some time passed, and eventually Jane felt ready to reach out, first to the church music teacher, and eventually to her minister. Her first meeting was with the woman who had taught her how to sing harmony. Jane was "reminded of the love I experienced back then, in that church." Some weeks later Jane was ready for the greater challenge of meeting her former minister and his wife. "I was so anxious," she said. "I did not want to be diminished for my alternative spiritual path." But as she watched them walk across the parking lot, "something in me shifted. I saw the reality of who they were, in the graying versions of those dear people who once were like family to me. I ran over and jumped into my minister's arms and for three hours we all talked, we remembered, we laughed, and reconnected to love on many levels. I had forgotten the love because I had focused for so long on my anger and pain." I was very moved by Jane's story and by the obvious joy in her voice as she described this reunion. And I was deeply gratified when she acknowledged that, "It was my 'zero' in Spiritual Growth that opened the door to my readiness to listen to Spirit and to find the courage to commit to opening up, over time, to a part of my past I was afraid to be with. It is true, I did need to go back, in some way, and allow healing to begin. I didn't even know this love was still in me."

I have heard many such stories over the years. Sometimes, there is nothing like the stark, inarguable reality of a number to propel one into action. Just as a low score on an exam in school indicates where you need to do extra study, a low score on this test can draw your attention to areas you may be unconsciously avoiding, as Jane was. Of course, a Spiritual Intelligence assessment presents a much more delicate and complex picture than a math exam, and it may take more than a little extra study to improve your score. But nevertheless, I have seen enough results to be convinced of its value. And, as soon as the more foundational piece of a skill is addressed and developed, scores rapidly jump, sometimes as high as a 4 or 5 on the 5-point scale.

Measure What Matters

My passion for measurement doesn't stop with the SQ21, and I encourage you to develop a fearless attitude towards measurement. With my corporate clients I always suggest that they measure anything that matters to them. I ask them for a list of all the things they care about: their goals, and the problems they are trying to address. Together, we figure out how we can measure the impact of the transformational work we are about to undertake on these different facets of their business. The more numbers we can put on the table, the better! One must be fearless about this kind of measurement, because the impact of working on seemingly intangible things like Spiritual Intelligence or Emotional Intelligence should show up in the tangible figures that affect a company's bottom line. The same is also true in personal settings. If you are genuinely growing as a person, you should see an impact in the areas that matter to you—in your relationships, your sense of well-being, your career. When you embark on a journey of intentional development—whether personal or professional—you should commit to looking for results in all the areas where you would expect to see an impact.

Some years back, I did a two-year initiative at one of the country's highest rated hospitals. I had been hired to do a values alignment, with the goal to make the hospital's culture more closely reflect the spiritual values stated in its mission statement. To track progress in this endeavor we used a values assessment by Richard Barrett.[18] But when I asked about the measures that mattered to them, the first thing that came up was nursing vacancy rates. One of their biggest concerns, they explained to me, was the shortage of nursing staff. Nurses were in such demand that when lured to a competitor by the promise of a signing bonus or a bigger salary, they would often leave the hospital after only a couple of years on the job. As a result the hospital spent a lot of money filling the gaps with temporary contractors, as well as on recruitment. Patient satisfaction was also a high priority for them—competition was high among the hospitals in the area and they had approximately two thousand beds to fill in order to meet expenses and continue their life-saving work.

When we began the engagement, we set out to track these measures and see if the values alignment would have an impact in these areas that were so key to the hospital's success. We tracked nursing vacancy rates, dollars spent on temporary contractors, satisfaction scores from customers and employees—every single business measure that they cared about. We also tracked values alignment through the values assessment. My belief was that values-alignment work would produce positive improvement on all those measures. And it did. Dramatic improvement was evident in customer satisfaction scores. There was a great reduction in nursing vacancy rates. The number of vacant beds went down. Contractor dollars dropped to zero because they had a full staff. Soon they got on the list of Fortune's "100 Best Companies to Work for," and have since moved up into the top ten. They proved that there is a direct relationship between the spiritual and the rational, between the intangible and the tangible, between the immeasurable and the measurable.

As you read this book and bring more focus to your own journey of becoming fully human, I would encourage you to start tracking whatever measures matter to you. Maybe they have to do with your personal well-being or health. Maybe they revolve around issues in your relationships, such as how often you fight with your spouse or find yourself irritated with your children. Maybe they are related to your self-esteem, your success in a chosen vocation, or your effectiveness in the workplace. Hold such measures lightly, knowing that multiple factors impact every situation, action, or interaction. But have confidence in the fact that your spiritual intelligence is a foundational factor that will, if developed, have a clear and visible impact in all the important areas of your life. Measurement is your friend. Measure fearlessly and grow freely.

PART TWO
4 Quadrants, 21 Skills

The 4 Quadrants and 21 Skills of Spiritual Intelligence

QUADRANT 1
Self/self Awareness

1. Awareness of Own Worldview
2. Awareness of Life Purpose
3. Awareness of Values Hierarchy
4. Complexity of Inner Thought
5. Awareness of Ego self/Higher Self

QUADRANT 2
Universal Awareness

6. Awareness of Interconnectedness of Life
7. Awareness of Worldviews of Others
8. Breadth of Time Perception
9. Awareness of Limitations/Power of Human Perception
10. Awareness of Spiritual Laws
11. Experience of Transcendent Oneness

QUADRANT 3
Self/self Mastery

12. Commitment to Spiritual Growth
13. Keeping Higher Self in Charge
14. Living Your Purpose and Values
15. Sustaining Faith
16. Seeking Guidance from Higher Self

QUADRANT 4
Social Mastery/Spiritual Presence

17. Being a Wise and Effective Teacher/Mentor of Spiritual Principles
18. Being a Wise and Effective Leader/Change Agent
19. Making Compassionate and Wise Decisions
20. Being a Calming, Healing Presence
21. Being Aligned with the Ebb and Flow of Life

FOUR

Know Thyself
(Skills 1 to 5)

"Make it your business to know yourself—which is the most difficult lesson in the world."

—Miguel de Cervantes, *Don Quixote*

Would you like to see less drama and ego in your home, your workplace, or your relationships?

When asked this question, no one says, "Oh, I love the rollercoaster of people's stuff. Give me more!" Most people just roll their eyes and say, "Oh my goodness, yes!" That's why I think of it as my "short answer" when people ask me: "Why do we need spiritual intelligence?"

At the heart of my Spiritual Intelligence (SQ21) model is a simple shift. In the opening chapter I raised the question, "Who is driving your life?" Spiritual Intelligence allows you to shift from being driven by the small-minded, short-sighted ego to being driven by the big-hearted, forward-thinking Higher Self. While you may not use these exact terms, I am sure you have some experience of noticing different parts of yourself. There is probably a part of you that you are not so proud of—that can be selfish, immature, defensive, and suspicious. And there is another part of you that may surprise you at times with its wisdom, kindness, and selflessness. I call these the ego and the Higher Self, or sometimes I just use a small "s" for the small self or ego, and a capital "s" for the big Self or Higher Self. You can use a variety of names for these different dimensions of yourself; I will share some suggestions later in this chapter. But to begin, if you can just relate to this simple distinction, then you have taken the first step on the road to Spiritual Intelligence.

Because the shift from the aspect of you we call "ego" to the aspect of you we call "Higher Self" is so central for SQ, the first of the Four Quadrants of SQ focuses on deeply *knowing yourself*—as Aristotle advised. Know who you are today and you can choose to work on who you want to become tomorrow. This self-knowledge is the foundation for becoming the wise, compassionate, and peaceful person you have the capacity to become.

So how do we do deeply know ourselves? The first of the Four Quadrants of SQ contains key skills for understanding yourself—knowing what makes you up, what matters most to you, and which parts of you need to be skillfully developed. Practicing the skills in this quadrant will help you become more aware of the difference between the big Self and the small self. That's why I call it Self/self Awareness. This quadrant contains five skills that are related to increasing your self-knowledge, sensing when ego is in charge, learning to hear the voice of Higher Self, and clarifying the personal intention, mission and values that reflect the very best parts of yourself. These skills are listed below.

Quadrant 1: Self/self Awareness

Skill 1. Awareness of Own Worldview

Skill 2. Awareness of Life Purpose

Skill 3. Awareness of Values Hierarchy

Skill 4. Complexity of Inner Thought

Skill 5. Awareness of Ego self/Higher Self

In developing the SQ21 assessment instrument, I have identified a series of levels for each of these skills, which range from 0 (no skill development yet) to 5 (mastery). While there is not the space in this book to describe all the levels in detail within each skill, I will endeavor to give you a sense of the range of development possible for each. To further illustrate the way the model works, I will choose one skill from each quadrant to lay out in greater detail.[19] For Quadrant 1, we will focus on Skill 5 on the list above. But first, let's examine each of the other skills related to Self/self Awareness.

Skill 1: Awareness of Own Worldview—
"What filters do I see through?"

The first skill in Quadrant 1 is Awareness of Own Worldview. What is a worldview? The simplest way to explain it is to reverse the two words that make up the term—it is your *view* of the *world*. The emphasis here is on the word "view," which in itself implies the most important thing about this skill: the recognition that the way you see is not simply "the way things are"—it is a particular *view*. The word "worldview" comes from the German *weltanschauung,* composed of the words for "world" and "outlook." It is commonly used to refer to the framework of beliefs and ideas through which we interpret the world around us. Those beliefs and ideas are inevitably going to be shaped by the culture in which you have grown up, your religious background, your ethnicity, and many other factors.

Worldviews refer not to *what* you see, but to *how* you see. N.T. Wright, a Christian scholar, clarifies this point when he says, "[Worldviews] are like the foundations of a house: vital, but invisible. They are that *through* which, not at which, a society or an individual normally looks."[20] You can think of a worldview as being like a contact lens, or a filter, that is so close to your eyes you are not usually aware of it. This filter works in two ways simultaneously. Firstly, a worldview filters *out* information that does not seem relevant to your view of the world. If you have a religious worldview, for example, you might be inclined to filter out information that conflicts with your beliefs. We see a clear example of this filtering out process in a small number of Christians who discount scientific evidence of the age of the earth in order to continue to see a world created by God in a literal (versus metaphorical) six days (in the Biblical account God rested on the seventh day).

Secondly, a worldview filters what you allow *in* to your awareness through interpretive layers. We might review a series of scientific studies but only cite those that agree with our position. This is a form of intellectual dishonesty. Most (but not all) of the time, this happens unconsciously. If we really value the truth we must fight against our tendency to exclude relevant data that disagrees with our established beliefs. A high-SQ person knows enough about herself to watch for this internal filtering process. She knows that everyone has filters and every perspective is an interpretation. As Ken Wilber puts it, "What our awareness delivers to us is set in cultural contexts and many other kinds of contexts that cause an interpretation and a construction of our perceptions before they even reach our awareness. So what we call real or what we think of as given is actually *constructed*—it's part of a worldview."[21]

You may be quite familiar with the concept of a worldview, but I have found that for many people, this concept can be both new and extremely helpful. Seeing how deeply a worldview is embedded and unconscious was mind-opening for me. It was truly a shock when I first realized that other people's brains might process information differently than mine processes it. Personality Type models, such as the Myers-Briggs Type Indicator,[22] can be helpful in understanding this. In Myers-Briggs language, I am an introvert with a preference for thinking style. That means I have an introverted way of processing information and I prefer to look at things logically. I like to be quiet and process information thoroughly before I speak. I was shocked to realize that extroverts think *by* speaking their thoughts out loud. What I tended to interpret as "yammering on with half-baked ideas that are a waste of time" were actually essential conversations for the extroverts in the room. They "baked" their ideas by talking them through with each other. My arrogance was in assuming their brains worked like mine. Of course, I can only experience what it is like to live inside my own brain. But it never occurred to me before I was trained that there was another way to successfully process information. Maybe you have made the same kind of assumption? Through the eyes of the extroverts, I realized that introverted people appear to be withholding, passive, arrogant, or non-participative. Ouch! Yet once we were all trained in the basic model of Myers-Briggs types, we could communicate without the handicap of that inaccurate assumption about each other. This was a successful illustration of the power of seeing one's own assumptions and lenses.

Of course, once we realize that we have different beliefs, assumptions, and interpretations (or worldviews), we can experiment with trying to look through the eyes of others and develop our spiritual intelligence in this way. But none of that can begin until we recognize the simple fact that we have a worldview. That awareness is what Skill 1 is all about. Awareness is foundational—that's why it comes first. You can't get outside of your current worldview and evaluate its usefulness until you notice you have a worldview!

Awareness of your own worldview is a foundational skill but also surprisingly easy to overlook. One example I often use to illustrate the importance of this skill involves something you probably think about rarely, if ever, but you negotiate every day. How far away do you stand from another person in a social setting? This is what is known as "social distance," and it is one of the unspoken but agreed upon rules that form part of your worldview, and the worldview of anyone who shares your cultural background. In North America, acceptable social distance is approximately eighteen to twenty-four inches, nose to nose (about an arm's length). Pay attention next time you are at a business conference or an office party, and you will probably see that most North Americans share this unconscious agreement.

Now, imagine that you are a North American female. A new person has come to work in your office. He has just been transferred in from a very different culture—Brazil, for example, or Italy. At the office reception held to welcome him to the team he comes and introduces himself to you, and stands very close, his face a mere six to ten inches from your own. You might feel some anxiety and take a step back without even thinking about it. Also operating from habit, he takes a step forward, closing the gap once again. You might wonder if he is hitting on you or you might feel intimidated or offended. Affronted, you break off the conversation. What you are not aware of, in this example, are two key pieces of information. Firstly, you are not conscious of the fact that your idea of acceptable social distance is not an absolute, hard-and-fast rule, but simply part of your particular worldview. Your perception that the new person is violating your space is an unconscious story you are telling yourself that has been told to you by the culture you come from. You don't consider that the transferee may hold a different worldview and have a different idea of what is socially acceptable. In fact, in his culture, six to ten inches is quite normal.

He isn't trying to hit on you or intimidate you; he is merely being friendly. But your withdrawal from the conversation has confused him, making him worry that he is not welcome in his new job. And you are not the only one who keeps stepping back and then breaking off the conversation. He's gotten the same response repeatedly throughout the evening. While you might feel angry, he might leave the reception feeling confused and rejected.

In our globalizing world, most of us have probably had this kind of cultural misunderstanding in one situation or another. What this example illustrates is how simply having an awareness of your own worldview—recognizing the fact that you have a worldview, understanding that your perspective is not simply "the way things are," and having some degree of objectivity on your own cultural biases and beliefs—can create the space to avoid a misunderstanding like the one described above. To make a difference in this skill, it is ideally co-developed with Skill 7: Awareness of Other Worldviews (we discuss this skill in Chapter 5). But we can start by just being aware of our own point of view. I find it best to introspect anytime I get annoyed by someone I meet or see on TV. I ask myself: "What interpretation am I making? What beliefs and assumptions are causing that interpretation?" Try it—you may be amazed at the space it creates for others.

Noticing your worldview requires some courageous introspection. It can be difficult to see our own assumptions. In the SQ21, I have traced the development of this skill from the most basic level, which involves being able to effectively describe your own belief system, through the more advanced levels at which you start to recognize that your worldview is not the only legitimate one, to appreciate its importance and its limitations, to develop humility about your own beliefs and, finally, to hold a nonjudgmental space in which you are not imposing your beliefs on others.

The science of worldviews is fascinating, and has been pursued in great detail by developmental theorists. Indeed, one very rich and powerful way to understand the evolution of human culture since the beginning of civilization is to study the way in which our collective worldviews have evolved.

Skill 2: Awareness of Life Purpose (Mission)—
"Why am I here?"

The second skill focuses on your awareness of your life's purpose, your mission, vocation, calling—whatever term you prefer. Clarifying your mission is central to self-knowledge—knowing not just who you are, but why you are here. As Marcus Aurelius, the second-century Roman emperor-philosopher, declared: "Everything—a horse, a vine—is created for some duty. . . . For what task, then, were you yourself created? A man's true delight is to do the things he was made for." That "true delight" is what I call my "joy paycheck," and it is as important, if not more so, than the cash paycheck I get each month. If I'm earning my cash paycheck but am impoverished when it comes to joy, I am not living a spiritually intelligent life.

Similarly, Abraham Maslow wrote in the twentieth century that, "A musician must make music, an artist must paint, a poet must write if he is to be ultimately at peace with himself. What a man can be, he must be."[23] Maslow saw the discovery and fulfillment of one's life-purpose as not just a source of delight, but as a "need" in the same way that hunger is a need. He termed this the need for "self-actualization," which "refers to man's desire for self-fulfillment, namely the tendency for him to become actually what he is potentially: to become everything one is capable of being." Another quote I love, from the Gospel of Thomas, cautions us against the dangers of not fulfilling our purpose: "If you do not bring forth what is within you, what is within you will destroy you." In other words, the dreams of what we might have done or should have done can sap the joy out of life and leave us filled with regrets in old age. The pursuit of a purpose-filled life, while it might contain hardships, can leave us feeling good at the end of our lives. I want to be able to say at the end of my time here: "That was a joyful life which served my loved ones and served the world."

Countless other great teachers, researchers, and thinkers have written on this topic, leaving us all with a rich library of contemporary and time-honored wisdom to choose from. Therefore, I will not spend much more time describing it here, except to say that in the SQ21, this skill is broken down into levels that begin with the simple aspiration to live in alignment with one's purpose, and develop through the ability to identify one's own gifts and talents, describe one's life-mission, examine one's choices and actions in light of that mission, and finally, at the highest level, to be stable in that mission in the face of great challenges.

Skill 3: Awareness of Values Hierarchy— "How will I choose my priorities?"

The third skill is about values, so we need to begin by defining that term. What is a value? Here's my chosen definition: A value is something you feel is important enough to base actions and decisions on. The reason I like this definition is that it makes the point that a value is something you act on. If you say that you value your health, but you don't eat well or take care of your body, then it is not a real value. At best, it is an aspirational value. Lived values, on the other hand, are backed up by choices and actions, and if we want to see our values, we simply need to look at the choices we make and the actions we take. "We can tell our values by looking at our checkbook stubs," said Gloria Steinem, succinctly capturing this point.

Ideally, your values should be consciously chosen, not simply handed down from those who came before. Initially, our values tend to come from our family of origin, and then at a certain point in life we often reject them in order to seek out our own consciously chosen values. Later in life, we may re-adopt the values of our family or culture of origin, but this time more consciously. An unconsciously held value, even if acted on, is not as strong a personal resource as one you have chosen. When push comes to shove, it's the values you have chosen—not passively received—that are going to hold you, stabilize you, and enable you to stay on course.

The SQ21 traces the development of this critical skill. At its basic level, you simply understand the importance of having values. You then develop the ability to know and articulate your values more specifically. You evolve a capacity to connect those values to your Higher Self, to order them in a hierarchy, and align with them easily, even if the consequences are difficult to see or cause sadness.

To begin shedding light on your own values, I suggest you start by making a list of everything you think you value, in no particular order.

Then review your list and try to eliminate those values that are merely unconsciously inherited, which hold no personal meaning for you. Aim to end up with a list of values that are *yours*—freely chosen and meaningful to you. Once you have this list, write each value on a card and see if you can rank them in order of importance.

Some people balk at this suggestion to rank or prioritize their values. Why is it necessary to create a hierarchy? The answer is that you have to make decisions on a regular basis, decisions that require that values-based information. Life often presents us with situations that cause two or more values to clash. They might be small decisions—should I go to my son's baseball game, even though it means cancelling a meeting with that important client I've been trying to sign for weeks? Or they might be big decisions—should I marry my sweetheart even though she is not from my religion and my church and family disapprove of this? Which value will trump the other?

When I first did this exercise for myself, I boiled it down to three values: God, Family, and Work, ranked in that order of importance. I realized that God came before family, because I did a "thought experiment." I imagined a situation where I had to choose between following the calling of my soul and making my family happy. I realized that if there was no way to do both, I would make choices and take actions that clearly put my spiritual work ahead of my family's preferences. I believed in my heart that I would make this choice even if that meant becoming estranged from one or more family members. Similarly, I put family ahead of work, because when I asked myself, "If someone in family really needed me, would I cancel a client engagement, even if it that meant a potential rupture with the client?" The answer was yes, if the family need for me was significant. Therefore, family trumped work.

Of course, we can't be overly simplistic about these matters, because they are often entangled with each other. A father might appear to choose work over family, missing his son's baseball games or his daughter's ballet recital. But he might argue that the only reason he works late so often is to support his family—to pay for the baseball coaching and the ballet lessons. Take these nuances into account in your own situation, but make the effort to rank your values as best you can. In those moments when you are called on to make a quick decision between two things that matter to you, knowing your values hierarchy makes an enormous difference.

I eventually added a fourth value to my "big three": my health. I became aware that if I didn't take care of my health I could compromise all of the other things that mattered to me, so I represented health as a circle enclosing the other three: I care for myself so I can fulfill my purpose and take care of my family and my clients.

Skill 4: Complexity of Inner Thought— "Can I handle the complexity of life?"

The next skill is called Complexity of Inner Thought. This may sound like something closer to IQ than SQ, but this skill is quite distinct from the logical and linguistic skill sets that are traditionally associated with IQ. Complexity of Inner Thought points to the ability to hold nuance and complexity. As an example, the first level of this skill includes the recognition that "rules are guidelines and sometimes a higher principle requires that I break the rules." Think about someone like Mahatma Gandhi—a very principled man, a lawyer in fact, who chose to violate the British law in order to support a higher principle. He was not randomly breaking the law for his own selfish gratification. He meditated for a long time before he decided that there was a more important principle at stake, and he was willing to go to jail and to suffer the consequences, including the possibility of death at the hands of the police or soldiers, in order to advocate for that principle. In everyday life, this skill asks if we are blindly obedient to authority, or if we can be law-abiding except when principle demands otherwise.

Higher levels of development in this skill take us into territory where we begin to develop the ability to consider multiple points of view in decision-making, and understand that "right" and "wrong" are not simple matters. Doctors, for example, need this skill on a daily basis. A patient is being kept alive in an ICU on the insistence of his family, even though there is no hope of his ever recovering. How does one weigh the ethics of honoring the family's beliefs with the ethics of providing that same bed to another patient who may need it right away? Your young adult daughter bristles when she is told what to do, but she wants to follow a career that entails physical and financial risk. You want her to choose her own path *and* you want to provide the necessary warnings and guidance. You want to support but not enable. How do you do all this?

As we progress to the highest levels of development in this skill, we develop the ability to recognize elements of truth in conflicting points of view, embracing and even enjoying paradox and mystery, which are central to mysticism. Holding the tension of opposites can create "third options" which creatively take everyone to a new level.[24]

Skill 5: Awareness of Ego self/Higher Self— "Who is driving my life?"

This skill is where we focus specifically on those two parts of the self: the ego and the Higher Self.

If you're not comfortable with the terms "ego" and "Higher Self," you can use whatever terms feel most authentic to you. For example, the Higher Self can be called your Inner Wisdom, Spirit Self, Soul, Essence, Eternal Self, Atman, Buddha nature, the Divine within, the Tao within, and so on. The ego can also be called the small self, the personality self, the temporary self, the limited self, or the lower self. Whatever names you choose, you should be able to identify these two parts of your self. We all instinctively know what ego looks like, by whatever name we call it, and we know what effect it has on our ability to live and work together effectively, harmoniously, and creatively. We all know what it's like to have a friend who seems so wound up that everyone tiptoes around him. Or to be part of a family that just can't seem to agree on anything. Or a coworker who just seems to go out of her way to be contentious. And whether we like to admit it or not, we know that there's a part of ourselves that sometimes gets us into this kind of trouble. This aspect of ourselves can be selfish, immature, fearful, and defensive, and it causes many of the problems we have when we attempt to collaborate with others. Where there is drama, you can be sure there are two or more egos interacting.

Similarly, we all have some sense of a better part of ourselves—a "Higher Self" or most authentic self. It's the part of you that is unselfish, loving, and wise. I like to say that when I'm operating from my Higher Self, nothing I do would embarrass me if it were printed on the front page of the newspaper, because I would be operating, to the best of my understanding, from the intention to be a loving person in the world. Once we agree that we each have these two aspects of self, we can then understand the basic practice of developing spiritual intelligence. The bottom line is that if you're going to be more spiritually intelligent, you need to act less from your ego and more from your Higher Self. And in order to make that shift, you first need to learn to identify the "voices" of the two different parts of yourself. That is what Skill 5 is all about.

Changing behavior starts by first increasing Self/self awareness. So Skill 5 is about shifting your attention from the voice of your ego self to the voice of your Higher Self. Most of us experience the voice of the ego as the dominant voice inside our heads. Think about this for a moment: When you are driving along the road after work, do you sometimes engage in a conversation with yourself? Most people will chuckle and admit that they do. One part of you is probably frustrated, angry, or impulsive, while another wiser, calmer voice tries to reason with your self. It is a completely normal human experience to have this sensation of arguing with oneself. In fact, there's a whole psychology of voice dialogue that encourages people to interact with these different voices. From a Spiritual Intelligence standpoint we want to look at two voices in particular: the voice of the ego self and the voice of the Higher Self.

A word of caution, as we look more closely at this particular skill. Ego is a very complex concept, and it is all too easy to get bogged down in all kinds of arguments about what ego means, its positive aspects, and so on.

Ego is used in the spiritual literature to refer to our separated sense of self as a personality in a body who ultimately sees him or herself as disconnected from the rest of life. The great spiritual traditions have long spoken about this "enemy within." The Sufis talk about the nafs *ammara* or "tyrannical ego"; the Christians warn us against the mortal sin of pride. In the ancient Vedantic teachings we find references to the "deadly serpent," while Judaism tells us to be wary of the *yetzer harah*, our evil inclinations. The traditions offer us paths and practices to uproot and transcend it, and some go so far as to declare all-out war on the ego, declaring that it must be killed or destroyed. If that language sounds harsh or outdated to you, don't worry: This is not the approach of Spiritual Intelligence.

I am not advocating getting rid of the ego. Nor do I make it "the enemy." It is a necessary part of us that has helped us evolve as far as we have, and it contains many functions that are useful and needed in the world. Psychologists have contributed enormously to telling this story, showing how the ego is necessary for the integration of the self, and helping us to understand how it has developed over time. Psychologically speaking, the ego self sometimes has synonyms like "the persona" or "who I think myself to be," or "my self sense." And there's a whole complex reality around ego development that has been studied and mapped by developmental psychologists.[25]

Those who argue that we should not "demonize" the ego are right— it would be like demonizing our left arm. The ego is a necessary part of who we are. But we should not use such arguments to avoid the simple but sometimes uncomfortable fact that there is a part of each one of us that is—at least at first—less mature or selfish or fearful or angry. Unless we have done a lot of personal growth, our ego is generally providing a partial and ultimately unsatisfying view of life. We need to mature our ego and place it in service to our Higher Self. As we do this, we are actually moving into the higher stages of "ego development." Therefore these systems—the psychology of ego-development and the practice of SQ—take us to the same destination.

To keep it simple, I like to think of our "ego" as our "self-identity." Who do you think that you are? How do you describe yourself? Do you remember, as a child, how people often asked: "What is your favorite color?" They were helping you to see that what you like might be different from what others like. I might prefer blue while you prefer yellow. What does that mean? There was some "self" called Cindy that had preferences. School taught us what we were good at, and what we weren't good at. "You are very good at math," you may have heard, but maybe you also heard, "You are not so good at sports." Our sense of who we are and what we are good at is part of our ego-development process. There is *someone* there—a separated "I"—a person with a name and traits and preferences. And we learn to defend that self. I remember a big battle in fifth grade between the kids who thought The Beatles were the best musical group, and those who defended the first manufactured "boy band," The Monkees (yes, I am showing my age!). In that process of defending my preference, I was also defending my sense of myself, and making others' way of doing or being "not for me." In so doing I began, as we all do, a healthy journey toward individuating, separating from family, choosing a career, and developing an early sense of who I was.

Let's pause here for a moment and admire the beauty of nature's process. The fact that we individuate at all is amazing. Developmental theorists tell us that this very capacity is a fairly recent emergence in human history. Our ancestors—and many people in less privileged circumstances around the world today—did not see and experience themselves with the same heightened sense of individuality that we take for granted. How much the world is served by the innovation and creativity that emerges from the early independence-focused periods of our lives! Yet this immature ego quickly gets "too small." By our late 20s or 30s we are usually feeling the pinch of it. We need to learn how to cooperate, to listen, to break down the barriers between me and you. Being "right" all the time is exhausting. The next steps for the ego are to mature, with EQ and SQ, to a place where we can embrace larger truths and multiple perspectives. In that process we discover the need to listen to the Higher Self.

Looking at this from a brain-science basis, we can consider that the ego (especially in the pre-conventional and conventional stages)[26] is fear-based. That is to say, it is highly connected to an "older" portion of our brain—our limbic system, which contains our "fight or flight" system and exists to keep us safe. It's really not that interested in whether or not we are happy or productive! Because the ego's primary goal is to keep us

safe and to keep us alive, it is always looking for what is "wrong" or potentially threatening in the situation or another person. This fear-based way
of perceiving activates the release of high levels of fear-related hormones
such as adrenaline and cortisol. Excessive fear-activation robs us of joy
as well as leadership capacities. Ample evidence now exists to prove that
when we experience significant limbic-system activation—when we are
triggered by fear—the blood flow in our body changes. Blood is redirected
to our fight-or-flight systems—our lungs, heart, and muscles. Blood is
directed *away* from "non-essential functions" (those that are not crucial
for fighting or running), such as digestion, reproduction, and higher brain
function in the neocortex. We literally lose IQ points when we are activated in fear. We have probably all had moments when we got triggered, and
said or did something that was totally "out of character" for us. In the
coaching world, we jokingly call these "career-limiting moments"—the
times when you rage at the boss in public or hang up on the company's
biggest client. It is the same in families. We often get triggered at major
family events such as holiday celebrations, graduations, weddings, and
funerals. Someone says the "wrong thing" and pushes one of our buttons, and we let him have it—often with consequences that go on for
years, decades, or for the rest of our lives.

The Higher Self, on the other hand, is far wiser than the ego self and
more expansive in its view. The Higher Self has a calmer voice. It can
calmly observe all the craziness of our life. It can even calmly watch our
own ego doing "its drama thing" and patiently smile. It has a longer-term
perspective, as well as the all-important ability to easily understand the
worldviews of others, a skill that we will be discussing in the next chapter. Pay attention to this voice in your own experience, and notice how
different it is from the voice of your defensive, reactive ego. Once we can
recognize that we have multiple "voices" or perspectives inside our own
self and that some of them cause us to act in ways that are undermining to our own development and that of others, then the spiritual journey—and the development of the other SQ skills—can begin in earnest.
As you develop Skill 5, not only does this distinction become clearer to
you, but eventually that calm, wise voice becomes the dominant one
that you hear.

Because Skill 5 is so foundational, I take time here to describe it in greater detail than the others while illustrating the five-level scoring system that is used for each skill in the SQ21 assessment. The levels for Skill 5 are illustrated in the table below.

1	I have a basic understanding that an ego self exists and that how it reacts to things is a result of my personal experiences since birth, including the influence of my family and my culture.
2	I can observe my own ego in operation. I understand there is a difference between the desires of my ego and of my Higher Self.
3	I can recognize the situations and types of people that trigger my ego self to want to take charge. I recognize the signals my body gives me when my ego has been triggered.
4	I can consistently hear the voice of my Higher Self. This may be a "felt sense" in the body, or an auditory or visual experience, or a combination. I may not hear it often, but I know it when I do. I am learning to listen to it. I understand how my thoughts and beliefs are creating the anger or fear I feel.
5	The voice of my Higher Self is now the principal voice I hear. Ego is now in joyful service to Spirit. I no longer feel a "tug of war" between these two parts of myself.

Let's take a closer look at the five stages or the five levels of skill attainment for Awareness of Ego self/Higher Self.

Level 1 skill attainment simply means **I have a basic understanding that an ego-self exists and that how it reacts to things is a result of my personal experiences since birth, including the influence of my family and my culture.** To attain this level, you don't have to do anything about the ego or change the way you relate to it. You don't even have to be able to see it clearly or recognize its voice. You simply have to cognitively understand and acknowledge that it exists. It's not a big step, but it is a significant one. Many people are not willing to admit this simple fact, and if you can't admit to having an ego you will never be in a position to grow beyond its influence.

Level 2 skill attainment builds on level 1 by bringing in a higher level of self-awareness. Now I not only admit that ego exists, but **I can observe my own ego in operation and I understand there is a difference between the desires of my ego and my Higher Self.** This is a significant step forward—when you can recognize ego not just theoretically but in your own self, and notice the difference between its voice and that of your Higher Self.

Level 3 skill attainment is a further step in which you not only observe ego in operation but you recognize the pattern of cause and effect that leads to ego-driven behavior. **I can recognize the situations and types of people that trigger my ego self to want take charge. I am aware of the signals my body gives me when my ego has been triggered.** The significance of this level is that your awareness is now occurring before the fact rather than after the fact, which is, of course, a critical step toward averting patterns of behavior and response that you recognize as less spiritually intelligent. At Level 3, you know your own triggers. You might become aware, for example, that issues around money cause your ego to rise to the surface. And you might see that when ego rises up, it expresses itself physically in the tightening of your jaw, a tension in your stomach, or a sense of strain in your neck. Pay attention next time you experience fear or anger. Notice how your body responds to those emotions. Physical symptoms are important clues as well as great helpers for increasing your self-awareness.

Level 4 skill attainment is a stage of development in which **I can consistently hear the voice of my Higher Self. This could be a felt sense in the body or an auditory or visual experience, or a combination. I may not hear it often but I know it when I do. I'm learning to listen to it. I understand how my thoughts and beliefs are creating the anger or fear I feel.** This is a high level of attainment, and not one that many of us can claim. But if we develop through the lower levels of this skill, we will find that we reach this rare degree of self-awareness. Often people will ask me, "How do I know it's the voice of my Higher Self and not the voice of my ego?" This is part of the self-awareness process—learning to recognize the difference. When you reach this point you won't have that question anymore. You know that voice without a doubt, even if you hear it only occasionally. Perhaps you identify it by a quality like peace, or space, or calm. I feel it almost as a different texture to the experience of being me. Some people experience their Higher Self as a kind of intuition, even an actual voice inside their heads telling them what to do in critical moments. Others see visions.

There is no right or wrong way to experience your Higher Self, but it is important to pay attention until you are sure that is what it is. And then you can learn to listen to it. This level of attainment also shifts our relationship to the ego. As we become more familiar with our Higher Self, we have the space to see how our own thoughts and beliefs are creating the anger or fear we feel. We can now understand that ego serves a useful purpose and that one of its purposes is to keep us safe. This is all deeply connected with our biological makeup—our limbic system and the functioning of our brains, as we will discuss in a later chapter. The ego creates the stories it does in order to fulfill its purpose, but it is not really concerned with our happiness or our spiritual development. As we become more aligned with the Higher Self we understand that we have the ability to interrupt the ego's story. But we can't interrupt the story if we are not clear about how our beliefs and thoughts are creating the fear or anger that we feel.

Level 5 skill attainment is the point at which **the voice of my Higher Self is now the principle voice I hear. Ego is now in joyful service to spirit. I no longer feel a "tug of war" between these two parts of myself.** When I say "the principal voice I hear," what that means is that the ego is no longer trying to drown it out. In the early stages of life the ego is the dominant voice. As we begin our spiritual journey, sometimes the ego gets even louder. But if we develop our self-awareness through the levels described here, by Level 5 the ego has calmed down and figured out its best role. The ego doesn't want to be destroyed; it wants to be important. And if you are intent on spiritual development, sooner or later your ego will figure out that the best way it can be important is to be in service to the Higher Self, because you have made it very clear that you are not going to listen to it in any other context. So at this level, ego finds a new purpose. Ego can now be important (something that is gratifying to it) by serving this higher purpose and mission that the self is committed to. The voice of the Higher Self is the captain, if you like, and the ego is a valuable team player. In this way the tug of war between these two parts of myself comes to an end.

Let's return, for a moment, to the metaphor of your life as a car. The goal of SQ development can be summed up as that point at which your Higher Self is driving the car and ego is simply the navigator. And it is important that ego is the navigator—it has not been thrown out of the car or shut in the trunk. My belief is that the ego is a healthy and natural aspect of the self, as adult development theory has shown us. We need the ego to be mature and we need the ego to be present in order for us to navigate the world. From a theological or philosophical standpoint you can think of the Higher Self as the part of you that is connected to what is universal and timeless—the part of you that has a big perspective on life, but may not understand the details of how to navigate the complexities of everyday existence. You need the ego present and mature to help you interface with other embodied people. As long as we are in our bodies, we need our egos. Your ego is able to detect what is going on with other egos. To not have an ego to navigate would leave you driving blindly. Without your ego self you would be well-intentioned but not skillful. To be both well-intentioned and skillful, you need these two parts of the self to be good partners.

That partnership—of mature ego plus Higher Self—is where all of this development is leading. And it is a significant attainment for any human being. The skills in Quadrant 1 that we have discussed in this chapter lay the critical foundation of self-knowledge upon which you can develop the mastery over yourself that is needed to reach the described goal.

Quiz: Consider Your Development of Quadrant 1 Skills

For each question, decide if your current skill development is low (L), medium (M), or high (H). While this is not a validated self-assessment, it may give you some idea of your priorities for personal growth. (To take the full SQ21, a carefully created, researched, and validated assessment, go to www.deepchange.com.)

Skill	Question to guide you	L	M	H
1. Awareness of Own Worldview	Do you feel that you can explain to others the impacts of your culture, your upbringing, and your mental assumptions on how you interpret the world around you?			
2. Awareness of Life Purpose	Do you feel that you can explain your life purpose to others? Do you stay focused on it consistently?			
3. Awareness of Values Hierarchy	Can you name and rank your top 5 personal values? Do you keep them in mind when making important choices?			
4. Complexity of Inner Thought	Can you hold conflicting perspectives on the "right thing to do" simultaneously? Can you make decisions in the face of uncertainty?			
5. Awareness of Ego self/ Higher Self	Can you consistently hear the voice of your Higher Self?			

FIVE

Know The World
(Skills 6 to 11)

*"Compassion is based on a keen awareness of the
interdependence of all . . . living beings, which are all
part of one another, and all involved in one another."*

—Thomas Merton,
addressing a monastic conference
in Thailand, December 10, 1968

In the second of the four quadrants in the SQ21 model we continue the theme of awareness, but now I will ask you to lift your eyes from the contemplation of your own self and turn your attention to the world around you. What do you see? And *how* do you see? Spiritual Intelligence is about learning a set of skills that can help you navigate the world with greater wisdom and compassion. Before you can navigate the world, you need to understand the world. That is what the skills in this quadrant focus on. I have chosen the term "Universal Awareness" to encompass the breadth of the skills that this quadrant includes. Consider the following questions: How broad is your perspective? Are you able to see the world from the perspective of another person or another culture? How far can your imagination stretch to envision the history of the universe or its dimensions? How aware are you of the interconnectedness of life and the spiritual principles that underlie it? All of these questions can act as portals into the skill-set that I call Universal Awareness.

As I did with the first quadrant, I will walk you through the skills of this second quadrant and focus in-depth on one skill in particular in order to illustrate the 5-level scoring system used in the SQ21. Among the six skills in this quadrant, I consider Skill 7, Awareness of Worldviews of Others, to be of the most immediate benefit. For this reason I have chosen to explore this skill in-depth.

Quadrant 2: Universal Awareness

Skill 6. Awareness of Interconnectedness of Life

Skill 7. Awareness of Worldviews of Others

Skill 8. Breadth of Time Perception

Skill 9. Awareness of Limitations/Power of Human Perception

Skill 10. Awareness of Spiritual Laws

Skill 11. Experience of Transcendent Oneness

Skill 6: Awareness of Interconnectedness of Life

Albert Einstein wrote in a letter to a grieving friend that, "A human being is part of a whole, called by us 'Universe,' a part limited in time and space. He experiences himself, his thoughts and feelings, as something separated from the rest—a kind of optical delusion of his consciousness. The striving to free oneself from this delusion is the one issue of true religion."[27] What Einstein states so beautifully is a truth that more and more of humanity are waking up to: the fact that we are not isolated islands, but rather we are threads in a vast web of interconnectedness. Martin Luther King Jr. described it as being "caught in an inescapable network of mutuality, tied together into a single garment of destiny."[28] The movie It's a Wonderful Life, in which an angel shows a frustrated businessman what the world would have been like if he had not existed, captured this truth in such a moving story that it became a classic.

This simple but profound message is one of the core tenets of all the great wisdom traditions and has been powerfully expressed by mystics, poets, and philosophers for millennia. For human beings at the beginning of the twenty-first century, interconnectedness is no longer a mystical metaphor or a romantic idea. It is a reality that we confront daily, in very practical matters.

We now know what our forefathers and mothers were not able to know: that our simple, everyday choices, such as the kind of car we drive, how we dispose of our waste, or the products we purchase, directly affect people and places we may never have any direct contact with. We can turn on the television and see images of polluted rivers clogged with plastic bags, mountains of electronics refuse in China, or sweat-shop laborers in the developing world producing goods for us to buy. We are increasingly offered options to be more conscious—to buy ethically, to recycle, to conserve energy. All of these reflect a growing awareness of the truth of our interconnectedness, with each other, with all of life, and with the planet that is our home.

Modern science is now increasingly able to demonstrate what mystics have always intuited. The relatively new discipline of ecology is one of the most obvious scientific expressions of the interconnectedness of biological life. Other sciences have also made breakthroughs that are less easy to grasp but even more extraordinary in their implications. Quantum physics, for example, has shown that "twin" photons, when separated, maintain non-local connections with each other even over long distances. The twin-photon experiment performed in 1997 by Dr. Nicolas Gisin and his colleagues at the University of Geneva demonstrated the mysterious long-range connections that exist between quantum events. Gisin sent pairs of photons in opposite directions to villages north and south of Geneva along optical fibers like those used to transmit telephone calls. Reaching the ends of these fibers, the photons were forced to make random choices between alternative, equally possible pathways. The results showed that the paired photons always made the same decisions, even though no explanation could be found in the laws of classical physics that would allow for such "nonlocal" coordination/communication. Many people see this kind of "quantum entanglement" as evidence of the deeper, underlying interconnectedness of life.

On the fringes of science, and in the increasingly populated territory where science and spirituality meet, all kinds of experiments are seeking to demonstrate the power of prayer, intention, healing energy, and other such intangible forces to affect physical objects at great distance. Beyond the specifics, what all of these paths of inquiry lead to is a greater awareness and appreciation for the multilayered interconnectedness of life.

This awareness is one of the foundational skills of Spiritual Intelligence. In fact, Fritjof Capra, the acclaimed physicist and systems theorist, defines "spiritual awareness" as "an understanding of being imbedded in a larger whole, a cosmic whole, of belonging to the universe." With this awareness there can be genuinely wise and compassionate action, because we deeply see that what we do to each other, what we are doing to ourselves and to our environment.

In the SQ21, we start measuring this skill from the most basic level, which involves respect for human life and empathy for others. The more advanced levels involve respecting organic life and animal life, understanding and feeling connected to the earth as a living ecosystem, and making choices to live a sustainable lifestyle. At the highest levels this skill becomes more challenging as we get into territory that demands more humility and complexity of thinking, as described in Skill 4. Can you appreciate, for example, that natural systems are complex and even chaotic and that seemingly destructive events such as forest fires may in fact be essential for the health of an ecosystem? Even some people who have made it their life's work to protect our national parks fall short of this level of awareness, as evidenced in areas where fires were excessively suppressed and caused the natural ecosystem, which relies on fires to clear out the underbrush to allow seeds to sprout, to be disrupted. Often we think we understand the interconnectedness of nature but we discover that we don't. Who would have predicted that wolves being reintroduced into Yellowstone National Park would have the most positive impact on the aspen trees? The wolves controlled the elk population that had been eating the aspen shoots.[29] Studying examples like this can help us to develop humility and complexity of thinking in relationship to the interconnectivity of all life.

At the very highest level, the SQ21 asks if you believe the universe is not only an interconnected system, but an intelligent system. You may choose to call that intelligence God or some other name or you may give it no name and just consider it "Life," but whatever you call it, acknowledging that interconnectivity and intelligence is the most advanced expression of this critical skill.

Skill 7: Awareness of Worldviews of Others

Skill 7, as I have said, is perhaps the most important skill in this quadrant. It is very closely related to Skill 1: Awareness of Your Own Worldview. As previously noted, a worldview is the framework of beliefs and ideas through which we interpret the world around us—beliefs and ideas that have been shaped by the culture in which you have grown up, including your religious background, your ethnicity, and many other factors. It is the lens through which you look at the world. And once you have gained the foundational awareness of your own worldview, you are in a position to understand and appreciate the worldviews of others.

How can we increase our understanding of other worldviews? Cross-cultural exposure is one of the most effective ways. One example I always like to use to illustrate that different worldviews can be literally worlds apart, involves burial rituals. Burial of the dead, in one form or another, is one of the defining characteristics of our species. The relics of ancient burial sites are one of the first signs that anthropologists use to draw the line between our hominid ancestors and the emergence of a race that could be called human. And yet the way in which we bury our dead varies dramatically from culture to culture.

When a U.S. soldier dies overseas, we (Americans) go out of our way to retrieve the body, even if all we can find are the bones and teeth, so that we can give him or her "a proper burial." We are still looking for bones in Vietnam. In the traditional Christian worldview that is dominant in the U.S., there is no closure without a proper burial, which generally means we take the body to a funeral home where they drain the blood, preserve the body, dress it in pretty clothes and apply makeup, and then we put it into a casket, and we put that in the ground inside of a concrete sarcophagus, cover it over with dirt, and put a granite headstone on top of it. That's a "proper burial." The family now has a place to go and talk to their beloved and put flowers on the grave.

Now let's consider another perspective on what a "proper burial" might mean. In Tibetan Buddhism there is a tradition called a sky burial. The first time I heard about this, it was quite startling to me and really caused me to confront the bias of my own cultural worldview. In the Buddhist system they believe that the essence of a person (we might call it "the soul") doesn't leave the body immediately, so burial does not typically happen until at least three days after the cessation of breathing and heartbeat. Sometimes the wait may be as long as forty-nine days if the person was a monk. On the burial day the body is taken before sunrise to a stupa, a sacred site containing a holy relic. There are certain stupas set aside for sky burials. The body is naked and wrapped in linen. At the stupa, at sunrise, a monk chops the body into pieces and places it on the shelves of the stupa for the vultures and other carnivorous birds to come and eat there. They take the bones that are too hard for the birds to eat and grind them up, add some grain, and scatter them around. The birds know what is happening, and they come and wait for the meal, so it is all over very quickly.

The first time I read about this practice I felt an instinctive revulsion. As a world traveler since early childhood I was puzzled by my own reaction. In thinking about it I realized that was simply my Western Christian upbringing—my inherited cultural worldview. From the Tibetan Buddhist perspective, it's a beautiful ceremony. They see one circle of life, and believe that once the essence of the person has left the body it needs to be returned into the circle of nature. It is also a much more practical solution—Tibet's landscape consists of very rocky terrain that would make burial difficult. Another advantage of giving the body to the birds is that the birds have a meal for the day and won't have to hunt. If you believe in reincarnation, which the Tibetan Buddhists do, it means that any mouse in the fields could be the reincarnation of someone you once loved. So by feeding the hunting birds with your body or the body of a loved one, you save that precious mouse-life to live another day. Once I understood the worldview that created it, I came to see sky burial as a profound and beautiful ritual—full of humility and an appreciation of the interconnectedness of all life. I tried to imagine what the Tibetans would think about the way most Christians handle a body in America. I could see how it would look crazy to them—wasting all that raw material and all that beautiful land and all that money and withholding the body from the cycle of life. They would see the form of burial I was raised to see as "proper" as deeply unnatural.

I love turning my world upside down whenever I can find an example like this. I truly find this to be fun! If you want to challenge your established worldview and learn to understand and appreciate the worldviews of others, find examples that really shock you. That contraction or repulsion is a sure sign that your hidden cultural biases have been triggered. Try to see the "shocking" behavior or tradition from the perspective of the people who live in those cultures. You will simultaneously gain compassion for others as well as greater self-awareness, both of which allow you to choose your own worldview more freely. In this way, skills 1 & 7 are very closely related, and develop in tandem.

Let's look more closely at the five levels by which we measure this skill in the SQ21. These are listed in the chart below:

1	I listen to differing points of view, even when they oppose mine.
2	I seek opportunities to learn about and understand other points of view.
3	I understand other people's points of view and "tune in" to their feelings even during a conflict. I want to understand their thoughts AND their feelings.
4	I have compassion for the hopes and fears that we all share, regardless of our worldviews. I can demonstrate to people that I understand their feelings. I have considered the many possible worldviews and have chosen a worldview from which to operate.
5	When I learn a better way of looking at things I revise my own worldview. Through compassionate understanding I can put myself inside the worldview of anyone—including murderers and terrorists. Other people feel that I really do understand their point of view.

Level 1 states, **I listen to differing points of view, even when they oppose mine.** This is a simple enough skill, but not something we can take for granted. Do we really listen to opposing perspectives, or are we already dismissing them in our mind, fortifying our own point of view? Next time you are in a debate or discussion, pay attention to the quality of your listening.

Level 2 states, **I seek opportunities to learn and understand other points of view.** This is a more active, intentional level of engagement with the skill, which demonstrates a growing awareness of the limitations of one's own worldview and the importance of learning about others. Engaging with other cultures, either through direct exposure, if you are lucky enough to have the opportunity to travel, or through reading and other media forums, is a great way to pursue this skill.

Level 3 states, **I understand other people's points of view and "tune in" to their feelings even during a conflict. I want to understand their thoughts AND their feelings.** Learning to "tune in" to the feelings of others as well as understanding the way they are seeing helps us to develop both empathy and compassion. This moves us from a head-based understanding to one that includes our heart. Empathy is the ability to feel what another person feels. Compassion goes a step further—while you feel what the other feels, you don't get lost in the feelings. Informed by wisdom, you have a loving desire to alleviate the suffering of others. Even two well-intentioned people can be in conflict when they are trying to make sense of a situation or the right action to take. Being able to remain open to other worldviews and the feelings of others, even during the heat of a conflict, is the goal of level 3.

Level 4 is quite an advanced attainment: **I have compassion for the hopes and fears that we all share, regardless of our worldviews. I can demonstrate to people that I understand their feelings. I have chosen a worldview from which to operate from among the many options I now understand.** Once you can appreciate the worldviews of others, it is yet a further step to see our common humanity beyond these cultural differences. The final part of this level is also an important one—now that you understand the multiplicity of worldviews, you are in a position to have freely chosen your own worldview. As we discussed with regard to values, those that are freely and consciously chosen have a much greater power than those that are unconsciously inherited. This does not mean you have to abandon the worldview that your parents and your culture have bestowed upon you, but it means you have examined it, questioned it, and freely embraced it as your own.

The highest level of attainment in this skill is Level 5: **When I learn a better way of looking at things I revise my own worldview. Through compassionate understanding I can put myself inside the worldview of anyone—including murderers and terrorists. Other people feel that I really do understand their point of view.** This is a very challenging level to reach. How can you put yourself inside the worldview of someone else, particularly someone whose actions you find abhorrent or incomprehensible? It starts with the understanding that if one person did those things, all of us might do it if the circumstances were the same. If we had the same biology, the same mental health problems, the same family and culture of origin, the same stimulus in our environment, and so on, as that person, any of us could potentially do anything that person did. One of the ways I think about this is that I am Mother Teresa and I am Hitler and I am everything in between.

Of course, I have free will, but in part, this is because I'm not a broken human being. I have led a fairly privileged life, I am educated, and I have a lot of resources available to me. Had I been born with Hitler's genes, his upbringing, his probable borderline personality disorder, and gone through all the other things that happened to him, I might very well have become who he became. It takes profound humility to reach that place where you authentically acknowledge, "I too could do that." It is not a very pleasant exercise to go through, but I find greater wisdom in the willingness to say, "I too could do that" than in saying "I would never do that." After all, which part of yourself would say, "I would never do that."? Most likely, it's your ego. Your Higher Self has more wisdom and much more humility.

Skill 8: Breadth of Time Perception

Skill 8, Breadth of Time Perception, is something you might not have really considered before. How big is your perspective, temporally? The ability to "think big" is an important spiritual skill, because the bigger the context in which you can see your own life, the more informed your choices and actions are. If you think of an extreme example, this becomes very obvious—someone who suffers from memory loss has no depth of time perception and keeps doing things over and over again as if it is the first time. She cannot learn from her own past or appreciate the impact of her choices on the future. As we consider our past we can see how it has shaped us. As we go further back, we can see how our parents were shaped by their parents and by the life circumstances of their childhood. My father was very affected by the Great Depression because his father lost so much during that time. His mom and dad really scrimped to feed eight children. During the aftermath of the Depression and through World War II, every child in Dad's family had to have a job as soon as possible. Usually that meant work began at age six. There was never enough money to feel secure. This changed how he saw the world. And it changed me, through him. I gain wisdom and compassion for him and for myself by seeing this.

Expanding this concept, we can see how human culture in general and our own nation-state in particular was shaped by world history. We can see how ideas transfer forward through time—and we can feel our responsibility to pass on only the best of ourselves to the future. My husband Bill and I often discuss how far the United States has come in our lifetime as far as diversity issues are concerned. We both joined Exxon in 1979 when affirmative action was relatively young and women's liberation conversations were in full swing. Prior to that time, a minority like Bill, or a woman, like me, would most likely not have been seen as management potential. Women who worked outside the home after having children were still a bit of a scandal in some circles. Sexist and racist jokes were prevalent. In just our lifetime we have seen so much change for the better. A woman or non-Caucasian person in management is no longer unusual. My daughter has trouble imagining the discrimination I tell her about from the time of my twenties. We have gone from the assassination of Martin Luther King Jr. in 1968 to the election of a black U.S. president in 2008. We have come a long way. And there is still plenty of room for improvement.

Let's "zoom out" even further. Consider the fact that only very recently has science been able to look all the way back to the birth of the universe. Human beings even a generation ago could not have seen their lives in a fourteen-billion-year context, but now we can. This is truly remarkable. We can see how from an explosion of hot gas came the galaxies and planets and eventually organic life. Contemplating the time-space enormity of the universe is both inspiring and humbling. Humility is a very important step toward unseating the ego, which likes to see itself as the center of the universe. If my lifetime is just the tiniest fraction of a fourteen-billion-year process that started with a vast explosion, it gives me quite a different perspective on the eighty or ninety years I may be here. When I feel like I need a humbling moment, I look at photos from the Hubble telescope and read about the enormity of space and time. No matter what I'm dealing with in my personal life, it snaps me into a different perspective, from which I can see on the one hand how insignificant I am in that context, and, on the other I can appreciate the grandeur and beauty of the whole evolutionary process. This skill helps me remain optimistic: I can see an evolutionary trajectory to the universe. It keeps me humble and less prone to take my life or my mistakes too seriously.

In measuring this skill we begin at a very basic level with awareness of one's personal history—one's own life and one's parent's lives. Then we slowly expand, looking at human history, the history of the earth, and the history of the cosmos. At the higher levels this skill also takes into account the ability to experience variations in our perception of time—moments of transcendent timelessness, as well as our ability to project the impact of our choices many generations into the future. So this skill requires complexity of thinking because it is paradoxical—it asks you to live your life knowing that your choices in every moment are very important (they may impact others today and far into the future) and at the same time that your life is an infinitesimally tiny piece of the whole story of the universe.

Skill 9: Awareness of Limitations/Power of Human Perception

Skill 9, Awareness of the Limitations/Power of Human Perception, is another very important skill that requires some complexity of thinking. The Buddha said, "Where there is perception, there is deception." We like to think, especially early in our lives, that our five physical senses are giving us an accurate and complete picture of reality. Understanding that there are things you are not able to perceive with your five senses is a foundation for humility, the first step toward spiritual behavior.

The greater your ability to appreciate that perception is inherently flawed, and to understand how your perception creates your own "reality," the more likely you are to act wisely. A simple way to begin thinking about this skill is to remind yourself that, for example, dogs can hear sounds you cannot hear and bats can sense objects in the dark that you would run into. Or think about the fact that we have invented x-ray machines to see beneath the skin of the body and microscopes to see bacteria and other objects too small for the eye to perceive.

Skeptics might say, "I will believe it when I see it." Yet often we cannot see what we are not expecting to see. In psychology it is called the phenomenon of "confirmatory bias." In other words, we look to see what we expect to see. If we dislike a politician we look for data that confirms our dislike—not data that disproves our hypothesis that his/her policies are flawed. In my coaching practice I often advise clients to seek *disconfirming* data. By setting their goal (thoughts) to feel rewarded by finding data that opposes the existing assumptions, their brain is more likely to "see it." This confirmatory bias plays a large role in optical illusions. We "see" based on our assumptions about how things work. We have trouble seeing what we do not believe in or expect or want to see.

This leads to a serious problem. We sometimes proclaim the truth by saying, "I saw it with my own eyes." Yet our eyes can deceive us. As you play with "optical illusion" puzzles[30] you can experience the disorientation that comes from watching your eyes "lie to you." Why would our brains be wired this way? Optical illusions illustrate the short cuts the mind takes to quickly assess or "understand" something. It is helpful to understand that the brain takes these shortcuts for a reason. Neuropsychology has shown that the brain has adapted to the need to make meaning quickly, and therefore it connects dots and fills in pieces that are not necessarily there. This is a tremendously helpful function in that we can quickly sense a pattern and perceive a possible threat. We can react quickly. Yet quick reactions are sometimes embarrassingly wrong. A good motto might be, "Don't believe everything you think you see." In other words, account for the reality that what the brain perceives is only partially true. Or as the PBS website says: "A person with perfect vision is still subject to optical illusions."[31]

At higher levels of this skill you learn to value intuition as a source of knowledge to help balance the flawed sensory process. You learn to marry these intuitive senses—which some might call spiritual insight—with your five physical senses.

Skill 10: Awareness of Spiritual Laws

In order to explain Skill 10, Awareness of Spiritual Laws, it is first important to explain what I mean by "spiritual laws." This language may make you uncomfortable—if so, you may prefer a term like "universal principles" or "spiritual principles." It doesn't really matter what words you choose, but it matters what they are pointing to. This skill is an inquiry into and an awareness of how things ultimately work. If you want to develop spiritual intelligence, it is important to have an experimenter's mind in trying to understand the interior and exterior worlds and grasp more deeply how things work.

Obviously in the "hard" sciences like Newtonian physics or chemistry, we have ways to prove universal principles. We can confidently state "the laws of chemistry" or "the laws of physics" (although even in these hard sciences humility is needed as new understandings constantly refine or even trump earlier ones). It gets harder to be so sure of how things work when it comes to sciences like quantum physics. But even this relatively esoteric science has some degree of testability, using complex mathematics and working with subatomic particles and accelerators and the like. However mysterious they may seem, the laws of quantum physics should not be over-simplified in order to be equated with spiritual laws. There is a tendency in spiritual circles to make claims such as "quantum physics proves x" or "quantum physics validates y" that generally involve some very loose science. Some interesting parallels may exist between these domains, but this is terrain in which I tread very lightly. When I talk about spiritual or universal laws, I am not going to make links to quantum physics.

I am a strong believer in the scientific method and in applying it to the world of our interiors. We can experiment with our thoughts and the results (for example, the emotional states) that they create. We can experiment with spiritual advice and see if it in fact improves the quality of our lives. In this I adhere to a teaching of Gautama Buddha from the *Kalama Sutta* regarding using your own good judgment and taking an experimental mindset. Scholars argue about proper translation, but this is my favorite version and one that I use as an internal guide on the topic of spiritual principles or laws. If you like it, you might want to adopt this stance as well:

> *Do not believe in anything simply because you have heard it. Do not believe in anything simply because it is spoken and rumored by many. Do not believe in anything simply because it is found written in your religious books. Do not believe in anything merely on the authority of your teachers and elders. Do not believe in traditions because they have been handed down for many generations. But after observation and analysis, when you find that anything agrees with reason and is conducive to the good and benefit of one and all, then accept it and live up to it.*

I define spiritual laws as spiritual rules, teachings, or ideas that either explain the right way to live or offer guidelines for how human beings can achieve happiness and inner peace. Spiritual laws, in the way I understand them, fall into the domain of *meta*physics, which basically means things that are beyond the laws of physics as it exists today—things we can't measure or explain yet. And the "yet" is very important here. There are a lot of things that are now solid Newtonian physics that weren't explainable a few thousand years ago, such as the basics of how objects of a certain mass interact with various forces (acceleration, friction, and gravity in particular) to move through space and time. Gaining this understanding enabled us to develop airplanes, rockets, and spacecraft that can travel to the moon and back. To our ancestors just a few hundred years ago, this would have looked like witchcraft. In the same way, things that are labeled "metaphysical" today may become ordinary science at some point in the future.

In the meantime, we must do the best we can to create and agree upon ways to measure and develop these intangible dimensions of life.

The SQ21 is part of my contribution to this endeavor. And the way I approach this often-confusing territory is to create two buckets for spiritual principles or laws: simple spiritual principles and complex spiritual principles. Simple spiritual principles tend to be more outer-world-focused and action-oriented. Included in this category are ethical teachings, rules, or commandments about what we should *do* in the world. "Thou shalt not kill" would be an example, as is the Golden Rule found in various forms in all the major religious traditions: "Do unto others as you would have others do unto you." Ideas about divine justice, karma, and redemption also fall into this category. Complex spiritual principles tend to be inner-world-focused and being-oriented. Complex spiritual principles tend to teach us how to *be* in the world. "Live in the ever-present moment of Now" is one such principle we often hear. Ideas such as "my thoughts have power," a belief in the healing power of prayer, or an awareness of synchronicity all fall into this category.

When it comes to spiritual principles, the SQ21 does not tell you what to believe. It asks you what you believe and encourages you to become more conscious and intentional about your beliefs. It also encourages you to experiment, to test your hypotheses, and come to your own conclusions. The basic philosophy I hold is that we should have an experimenter's mind with all of these spiritual principles, particularly the ones that are very difficult to prove. Rather than taking them on faith in a magical, simplistic way, I recommend that people examine them and experiment with them. So if you believe, for example, in some version of "the law of attraction"—that what you put your attention on you will draw toward you—try it. You might say that, "I believe that if I really focus on what I want, if I create a vision, write out a strategic plan, articulate goals and focus on them, the universe will provide opportunities around whatever it is I'm trying to accomplish." If you believe this, I suggest you test it. Do these things and then observe what happens in the course of a year.

When it comes to measuring this skill of Awareness of Spiritual Laws, the SQ21 focuses on how you are engaging with the spiritual principles you have identified rather than what those principles are. The most basic level is simply aspirational: "I want to live a spiritual life." As the levels progress, they focus on understanding the basic spiritual rules of your own tradition or culture, deepening your understanding of these principles by living them and observing the results, and at the highest level, your ability to apply them effortlessly even under stress.

Skill 11: Experience of Transcendent Oneness

The final skill in this quadrant focuses on the Experience of Transcendent Oneness. I have focused on this particular experience because it appears to be a near-universal element of religious and mystical teachings and paths, across the boundaries of time, culture, and place. As Ken Wilber writes, the mystics and sages "all tell variations on the same story . . . the story of awakening one morning and discovering you are one with the All, in a timeless and eternal and infinite fashion."[32] Aldous Huxley, who put forth the notion of a "perennial philosophy" common to many faiths, observed that all the mystical traditions point to "the more or less obscure intuition of the oneness that is the ground and principle of all multiplicity."[33]

Such experiences are often characterized as moments when Spirit "breaks through" the veil of ordinary consciousness and we see through the appearance of separation and multiplicity to the unity that lies beneath the surface. Such experiences can happen in all kinds of circumstances, not just on the meditation cushion. One example I love is the story of astronaut Edgar Mitchell who experienced a moment of transcendent oneness as he traveled back to Earth from the Moon:

> The biggest joy was on the way home. In my cockpit window, every two minutes: The Earth, the Moon, the Sun, and the whole 360-degree panorama of the heavens. And that was a powerful, overwhelming experience. And suddenly I realized that the molecules of my body, and the molecules of the spacecraft, the molecules in the body of my partners, were prototyped, manufactured in some ancient generation of stars. And that was an overwhelming sense of oneness, of connectedness; it wasn't "Them and Us", it was "That's me!", that's all of it, it's . . . it's one thing. And it was accompanied by an ecstasy, a sense of "Oh my God, wow, yes," an insight, an epiphany.[34]

Mitchell had experienced a moment of transcendent connection with all that is. His life was forever changed because of it. Some people experience this unity walking in nature, or in the arms of a lover, or witnessing the birth of a child.

Different traditions use varying language to describe these experiences, but in the end they seem to be pointing to the same truth. The philosopher William James, in his famous text *The Varieties of Religious Experience,* said this: "Personal religious experience has its root and centre in mystical states of consciousness."[35] Buddhists might speak of emptiness, Christians of Christ-consciousness or the Holy Spirit, Taoists of the all pervading Tao. Poets have found beautiful metaphors to communicate its mystery, such as the drop dissolving in the ocean or the sense of the entire cosmos becoming one's own body. However they are described, these profound, awe-inspiring moments of connection are deeply nourishing. Some of us may find we easily connect to this dimension while others tend more toward the concrete and rational and are less likely to access such experiences with ease.

The way we measure this skill in the SQ21 is to look at a graduated series of experiences and their frequency. The lower levels are things almost anyone can relate to—moments of "flow" or inspired creativity, where you are so focused on and absorbed by what you are doing that time seems to fly by, or "peak" experiences of unexpected pure joy. Such moments are baby steps in the direction of transcendent oneness—our habitual self-focus falls away for just a little while and we experience relief and freedom from the noise of the ego. The higher levels move from random experiences to regular experiences, and finally, to the ability to enter such states at will and integrate their wisdom into our life choices.

Universal Awareness

In Chapter 1 I defined spirituality as the "innate human need to be connected to something larger than ourselves—something we consider to be divine or sacred." The essence of this quadrant is connecting with that "something larger." We do this through relaxing our normal ego-boundaries, those boundaries whereby we defend our own narrow worldview. We begin to see the beauty of other worldviews. We grow more humble. We expand our sense of time and space. We can connect to the interconnectedness of all life as well as with a sense of awe and wonder at the vastness of the universe. And we learn to experiment with and live from a deeper set of spiritual principles than we might have lived from before.

From Quadrant 2 can come great art and poetry and great wisdom and compassion. While you might not choose to develop all of these skills, I encourage you to engage with all of them to see what attracts you. I think the powerful perspective-shifts that come from this can be the antidote to moments of sadness, or to times when you wonder, "Does my life have meaning?"

Quiz: Consider Your Development of Quadrant 2 Skills

For each question, decide if your current skill development is low (L), medium (M), or high (H). While this is not a validated self-assessment, it may give you some idea of your highest priorities for personal growth. (To take the full SQ21, a carefully created, researched, and validated assessment, go to www.deepchange.com.)

Skill	Question to guide you	L	M	H
6. Awareness of Interconnected-ness of Life	Do you feel the pain of (do you deeply empathize with) other humans and of animals who are suffering? Do you consider the consequences of your choices on ecosystems and future gen-erations?			
7. Awareness of Worldviews of Others	Do you seek to understand the emotions and perspectives of others even if you disagree with them? Do others feel under-stood by you?			

Skill	Question to guide you	L	M	H
8. Breadth of Time Perception	Do you consider the history that brought you to the worldview you have today? Can you hold a billion years of history in your mind and perceive an evolutionary trajectory in the universe?			
9. Awareness of Limitations/ Power of Human Perception	Are you aware of how your senses give you incomplete and sometimes inaccurate information? Do you supplement your five senses with intuition or spiritual insight?			
10. Awareness of Spiritual Laws	Do you think about and experiment with spiritual laws/principles? Do you try to live by your understanding of spiritual laws?			
11. Experience of Transcendent Oneness	Have you ever experienced a moment of awe, wonder, or non-ordinary consciousness? Has this experience of something transcendent helped you to focus on living from your Higher Self?			

SIX

Self-Mastery
(Skills 12 to 16)

*"He who is slow to anger is better than the mighty,
And he who rules his spirit, than he who captures a city."*

—Proverbs 14:29

*"He who controls others may be powerful, but he
who has mastered himself is mightier still."*

—Lao-tzu, Tao Te Ching

Self-mastery has always been a core precept of those who excel in any human endeavor. And throughout history it has been the bedrock of the great religious and mystical paths. Through meditative practices, austerities, disciplined training, and acts of renunciation, spiritual aspirants have sought to gain the upper hand over their human weaknesses, desires, and impulses. To be spiritually intelligent, we do not necessarily need to live like monks, give up all worldly goods, shave our heads and set out for the desert. But the principle of self-mastery is still central, because it is the means by which we give our Higher Self the upper hand over the often powerful drives of the ego. As author Dan Millman puts it: "Self-mastery occurs in those moments when we subordinate our little will—our personal tendencies and preferences—to the dominion of our higher will, Higher Self, higher integrity or higher ideals."

This quadrant comes after self-awareness in the SQ21 model, because we cannot master what we cannot see. In the Self-Awareness quadrant we talked about learning to identify your ego and Higher Self as well as clarifying your personal mission and values. This quadrant builds on those skills, teaching you how to shift ego out of the driver's seat and allow your Higher Self to take control. It teaches you how to live according to the mission and values you have chosen and how to stay centered and peaceful even during difficult times. As you put these Mastery skills into practice, you will find that they reflect back on the Awareness skills (Quadrants 1 and 2), deepening your understanding of who you are, your values, and the world around you. Peter Senge sums this up succinctly when he writes: "When personal mastery becomes a discipline it embodies two underlying movements. The first is continually clarifying what is important to us. The second is continually learning how to see current reality more clearly."

Self-mastery is not easy. But it is a skill-set that can be learned, through practice and conscious intention. The skills I have identified as components of self-mastery are listed below:

Quadrant 3: Self/self Mastery

Skill 12. Commitment to Spiritual Growth

Skill 13. Keeping Higher Self in Charge

Skill 14. Living Your Purpose and Values

Skill 15. Sustaining Faith

Skill 16. Seeking Guidance from Higher Self

Skill 12: Commitment to Spiritual Growth

Skill 12 is Commitment to Spiritual Growth. Commitment is foundational for any kind of development, and spiritual development is no exception. How do you measure commitment as a skill? In the SQ21 we focus on ways in which commitment to spiritual growth is demonstrated in action. For example, do you seek guidance from spiritual authorities, writings, and from people of different belief systems or traditions? Do you seek opportunities for growth? Do you make spiritual development a high priority in your life and demonstrate it by dedicating time and energy to its pursuit? Do you engage in multiple activities and disciplines?

This skill is an important one and one that can occasionally trip people up. Remember the story I shared in Chapter 3 about Jane and her "most precious zero"? It was this particular skill that produced this result and that eventually proved so transformative for her. Many people like Jane are surprised to find that they have a low score in this skill. Some are insulted and think it must be a mistake, claiming that they are deeply committed. And, in fact, they often have committed a lot of time and effort to their own development. When I or one of my trained coaches look more closely at such cases, invariably something is revealed that proves key to the client's growth. To understand why, we need to look a little more closely at the questions in the assessment that relate to this skill. One particular question seems to be the most common stumbling block. The assessment asks if you "seek to learn about spiritual topics from people, articles, books, or sacred teachings from within the belief system in which you were raised." And you have to answer at least "sometimes" to successfully complete this question. A lot of people are not able to answer "sometimes," usually for one of two reasons. The first reason is that some people don't think they were raised in a belief system and therefore assume the question doesn't apply to them. The second reason is that many people have unresolved issues and old wounds from their religion or belief system of origin, and therefore this is the last place they would seek for spiritual wisdom.

Both of these positions actually represent an obstacle to spiritual growth. You might call it an issue that is hidden or "in the shadow." In response to the first objection, I always say that everybody is raised within a belief system. Think about your parents or caregivers. What did they believe? Maybe they hated religion, and might be categorized as atheists, or secular humanists, or scientific materialists. Each of those labels still describes a belief system. Maybe they claimed to "believe nothing"—yet they acted in a way that showed their values and beliefs. Did they value scientific thinking and logic and disapprove of all the dogma and superstition that they associate with religion? What made them angry? Whom did they admire? These are all clues to the belief system of your parents, family, or caregivers. This comes back to the matter of worldviews that we have discussed at length in previous chapters.

We all have a worldview and we all have a belief system associated with that worldview. So recognizing your belief system of origin and entering into a more conscious dialogue with it can be a tremendous step in a commitment to spiritual growth. I have had clients say "Wow! I never thought about it like that!" and then generate a beautiful dialogue with their parents (if still alive) or other people who hold that view. This "ah ha" moment can lead them to "see" for the first time that they do hold a lot of assumptions based on their childhood. They may still be in agreement with those beliefs or they may be in opposition to those beliefs. If they are in opposition due to anger there is something waiting to be healed. This brings me to the second most common cause of a zero on this skill.

Even more common than not recognizing one's belief system of origin is a conscious rejection of that belief system as a result of old wounds. When I ask people who have done this about the belief system in which they were raised, I usually get a very specific answer. I was raised Jehovah's Witness. I was raised Southern Baptist. I was raised Roman Catholic. I was raised an Orthodox Jew.

It's interesting to me that people will often associate their belief system of origin with a very narrow denomination, even in some cases with only one minister or rabbi or spiritual teacher. The first step I ask people to take is to expand that frame. Rather than saying "I was raised as a Southern Baptist," they expand the context to say "I was raised as a Christian." The little piece of Christianity (or other religion) you experienced or that particular minister (or priest, rabbi, imam, or guru) may have been toxic, and you may have very wisely rejected that. But does that mean there is nothing you can learn anything from Christianity as a whole? Are there *any* Christians, living or dead, that you admire? You may not choose to attend a church, but is there anything that you can learn from Jesus? From Mother Teresa? From Desmond Tutu? As I ask questions like these, I usually see people visibly relax and even laugh, recognizing that they have confined all their ideas about their "religion of origin" to one very narrow association with a particular church or temple or individual. So they have cut themselves off from their roots rather than continuing to learn and grow.

I cannot overstate the power of these "ah ha" moments for my clients. Rifts with family members have been healed. Tears of joy have come streaming down the faces of people who realize that they can "go home" again in a new way. And clients have seen their belief system of origin with fresh appreciation and gratitude even if they are no longer interested in embracing its teachings. After healing wounds from the past and confronting shadows or "allergies" around it, I then focus on where the person would score if they were retaking the skill assessment with this new understanding. From that we can determine a next step for them as they continue to heal and grow.

Skill 13: Keeping Higher Self in Charge

Skill 13 is a critical skill because it is this skill that allows us to not only get the upper hand over our egos; it allows us to keep our Higher Selves in charge. Let's examine this skill in depth. The five attainment levels are listed in the chart below:

1	I can occasionally identify when I am acting from ego and I understand that acting on ego will not get me long-term satisfaction.
2	I am unhappy with how ego handles things. I want my Higher Self to be in charge.
3	I understand and can occasionally remember to use the skills to activate Higher Self and have it take over from the ego self.
4	I am consistently able to activate Higher Self and interrupt "ego moments." I am successful in keeping Higher Self "in the driver's seat" most of the time.
5	My Higher Self "muscle" has been developed by consistent daily practice for a long time—it is now a habit. Higher Self is in charge, even in profoundly trying times or under pressure from "group think."

The first level is the most basic level, which links us back to Skill 5 in the Self-Awareness quadrant—awareness of Higher Self/ego self. At the most basic level of skill development, you are able to say: **I can occasionally identify when I am acting from ego and I understand that acting on ego will not get me long-term satisfaction.** At the next level, not only can you identify ego-driven actions, but they begin to bother you: **I am unhappy with how ego handles things. I want my Higher Self to be in charge.** Level 3 takes a step further: **I understand and can occasionally remember to use the skills to activate Higher Self and have it take** over from the ego self. At this level you are beginning to attain some small but significant degree of mastery over yourself. This mastery increases at Level 4, where you can say, **I am consistently able to activate Higher Self and interrupt "ego moments." I am successful in keeping Higher Self "in the driver's seat" most of the time.** This is a high level of attainment. It is all too easy to recognize "ego moments" in retrospect, but to be able to interrupt them and allow the Higher Self to take charge before you have acted out of an ego-driven impulse or reaction requires a significant level of mastery. At the highest level, Level 5, this mastery becomes habitual, no longer requiring the kind of effort it may have taken at lower levels of development. **My Higher Self "muscle" has been developed by consistent daily practice for a long time—it is now a habit. Higher Self is in charge, even in profoundly trying times or under pressure from "group think."** Because of your consistent daily practice, Higher Self is like a muscle that has become strong and toned, making you prepared even for challenging times and pressured situations, or moments of fear, sadness, tiredness, and other emotions that would previously have triggered egoic responses. Of course, we are all human, so we may never get to the point where Higher Self is in charge 100% of the time, but a spiritually intelligent person who has worked hard on this skill is someone who can be counted on, even in bad times, to be choosing and acting on the very best part of themselves.

One key to this skill is understanding the relationship between thought, emotion, and action. This is why the skills in Quadrant 1 are so essential as a foundation. You need to know that certain ego-thoughts create emotional reactions, and that if you let such thoughts run rampant you will increase the emotional reactions that often include anger, blame, fear, and victimization. An essential part of self-mastery, of keeping the Higher Self in charge, is taking ownership of this process so that you short-circuit that egoic cycle. You learn how to interrupt the flow of ego thoughts and put your Higher Self in charge of your thoughts, words, and actions.

What does it take to keep Higher Self in charge? Events happen all the time in our lives that are beyond our control, and we have responses to these events in the form of thoughts, feelings, words, actions, and so on. For the most part our responses come from habit patterns. We are on autopilot. We have been programmed through the course of our lives, by way of a set of beliefs and worldviews, to interpret events in certain ways and to respond to them in certain ways. And many of those programmed responses are driven by our ego, which is trying to keep us safe.

"Not being able to govern events, I govern myself," wrote Michel de Montaigne. That is a spiritually intelligent approach. We cannot control the majority of the events in our lives. But we can control our responses. And the way we do that is by creating space between the things that happen to us and our reactions to them. When we are running on autopilot, we are not even aware of any space. There is just stimulus and response. But as we increase our awareness we become conscious of the tiny space that is already there and, most importantly, we can learn to increase that space. I call this "inserting a pause." It's the pause that contains your power. If there is no pause, you have no power. When you insert the pause, you create enough space between stimulus and response to be able to say, "Who is running the show here? Is my ego running the show or is there a wiser way that my Higher Self can handle this?"

In this way, you develop the art of conscious behavior. Think about your own behavior like a scientist would think about an experiment. Observe the external stimulus, your internal emotional reactions, and the arising of your "usual" autopilot response. Notice this process and then consider what the result will be. Do you like how that sequence of events turns out? Evaluate it. Then generate a new hypothesis. "I wasn't really happy about how that turned out. I wonder, if I try something new, might I get a different response?" And then the next time you run into a similar circumstance, choose based on your new hypothesis and see if you get a different result. Consider this an experiment. Observe the response, consider the result, try a new response, consider the new result. Eventually, you will get more skillful at having Higher Self responses to situations. What I find is that as I do this work it becomes a self-reinforcing loop. I like the results better. I feel better about how I handled the situation. Even if I didn't get something I "wanted" (or my ego wanted) out of the situation, I feel better afterwards. Therefore I am much more likely to make those choices again.

Another key to this skill, particularly as you develop into the higher levels, is forgiveness. Consider an example. Imagine you have a former spouse. This person did something you and all your friends agree was "unforgiveable." Let's say this person cheated—had sexual relations outside of your monogamous commitment. Why would forgiveness matter for keeping your Higher Self in charge? At the simplest level, you might have to interact with this person. You may share children, or live in the same small town. If you cling to the stories about how you were wronged, you will feel upset every time you see that person. You are more likely to snap at him/her or at other people who are around. To take it deeper, you are likely to transfer your woundedness into mistrust of others. This can damage your chance at having healthy, happy relationships in the future. And worse still, the unhealed wound may act like a leak in the bathtub of your joy—never really allowing you "fill up" with happiness over anything. That unhealed wound can keep you from fully embodying the best of who you can be.

So what is forgiveness? Forgiveness is not about forgetting what happened or saying the behavior or event was okay. It does not let a perpetrator of abuse "off the hook." In fact, *it is not even primarily for the perpetrator's benefit.* Forgiveness is "seeing a situation with new eyes." We do this as a gift to ourselves. Refusing to forgive is toxic. I heard this analogy somewhere: refusing to forgive someone is like drinking poison every day and hoping that eventually the *other* person will die.

Forgiveness calls heavily upon a practice called reframing—which we will discuss in Chapter 11. It is an essential practice for keeping your Higher Self in charge. When we cling to old stories we keep our ego in chronic agitation and in hypervigilance to avoid similar "attacks." This makes it very difficult to relax enough to seek your own inner guidance and choose a wiser or more spiritually intelligent response. I will show you how to practice reframing and forgiveness in Part III; this will help you hear the voice of your Higher Self more clearly.

Skill 14: Living Your Purpose and Values

Skill 14 builds on Skill 2, in which you identified your mission or life purpose, and Skill 3, Awareness of Values Hierarchy. Because spiritual intelligence is all about how we *behave,* simply having a sense of purpose and values is not enough. A spiritually intelligent person lives her life in accordance with her purpose and makes choices based on her chosen hierarchy of values. At the most basic level, living your purpose and values can mean having the ability to explain and describe them, first to other people that you trust and then in settings where people hold very different points of view. After all, if you are not willing to speak freely about your values even with those you trust, how committed are you to those values? As you develop this skill it requires that you make values-driven, purpose-driven choices even when no one else is around to know about it. If they really are *your* values, you hold to them when no one is watching and when there is no praise or recognition to be gained. At the highest levels you are stand by your values at significant personal cost. Think about your job, for example. Would you give it up rather than compromise your values? What about your family and friends—would you be willing to lose their support in order to stand by your values? The most challenging question that the assessment asks with regard to this skill is: Would you make values-based choices even when your own life may be at stake? Obviously that's a hard question to answer until you are faced with a situation that asks you to make such a choice. Some people I've worked with have faced and made this choice and can answer it with relative confidence. But I think we all have to have some humility around this one, because we don't really know. It's worth simply considering: at what point would I deviate from my values in order to survive? Survival itself is not a bad value, especially if others depend on you. Make a lot of room for the complexity and subtlety around these questions as you consider them.

Skill 15: Sustaining Faith

Skill 15 is Sustaining Faith, even during difficult times. If you are like me, you have probably experienced moments in your life where things seemed so unfair, so painful, so senseless, that you doubted whether there was any order in the universe. Life can feel purposeless, random, and cruel. We teeter on the edge of hopelessness. What sustains us during such profound pain? I would argue that there is a choice we have to make. Do we believe the universe has a purpose or not? There is a popular saying: "There are only two ways to live your life. One is as though nothing is a miracle. The other is as though everything is a miracle." This skill is about choosing to trust that *in the long run* life is purposeful, even when we cannot imagine what the purpose might be. This requires tremendous humility (supported by Skill 9) and an ability to hold a very large space and time horizon (Skill 8).

This skill is often most difficult for people who are atheists or agnostics. So let me turn to a secular resource to help us. In *Spiritual Evolution: A Scientific Defense of Faith,* George E. Vaillant, MD, describes what he has learned from thirty-five years of directing the Harvard University "Study of Adult Development," a famous seven-decade longitudinal study that has followed hundreds of men as they live their lives to observe what has helped them function well and what has not. Vaillant, a psychiatrist and professor at Harvard, considers in addition to psychology and psychiatry, the anthropological and neurological evidence and studies of animal behavior. He has come to believe that humanity evolved to be "programmed" for spirituality, saying, "Evolution toward spirituality takes place not only in the genetic and cultural arenas but also in the lives of every one of us as we mature."[36]

So what has this to do with sustaining faith in difficult times? Vaillant points out that while "pain, rage, and grief provide short-term benefits, positive emotions provide benefits over the long term."[37] He describes how humans have evolved with both the need for and the neurological ability to create the positive emotions of faith, love, hope, joy, forgiveness, and compassion. He points out that in the first thirty years of leading the longitudinal study he learned that positive emotions were clearly connected to mental health. He adds, "I have come to appreciate that positive emotions cannot be distinguished from what people understand as spirituality."[38] Later, he reflects, "If my purpose as an author can be oversimplified into a single wish, it would be this: to restore our faith in spirituality as an essential human striving."[39]

It is one thing to have faith in a Higher Power, or your own Higher Self, or the goodness of life when you feel inspired, confident, and on top of the world. It is another thing altogether to sustain that faith during times of difficulty, despair, fear, and uncertainty. How do you stay the course? Are you able to stay in relationship with a Higher Power—whatever name you choose to give it—during the challenges of life? Are you able to seek help and guidance when you need it? Some people have a negative reaction to the very idea of asking for help—feeling that it puts them in a powerless position or feeling that they have reverted to some kind of childlike relationship to a Daddy-God on high. As adults we do outgrow our "god images" from childhood. When we were five years old we might have seen God as a kind of benevolent Santa Claus who would grant our wishes. Or we might have seen him as an angry, punishing father. What typically happens as we grow cognitively is that we reject those childish images. The challenge, then, is to consider, what replaces those images? Is there any purpose or power behind life? Or is it completely random and meaningless? And if it has a purpose, do I have to understand it to believe that it exists?

I personally believe that seeing life as miraculous, intelligent, and "larger than me" is important to sustaining faith. A willingness to engage, humbly, in some form of surrender to the power of Life, to "all that is," is an essential aspect of sustaining faith in hard times.

In my approach to spiritual intelligence the idea of a Higher Power is important for this reason. But how you choose to define that power is completely up to you. SQ is not a particular belief system—it is, as I often say, both faith-neutral and faith-friendly. That means that if you do not have religious beliefs, that's fine. For you, a Higher Power might be the life-force of the universe, or the quantum field, or even your own Higher Self. If you do have religious or spiritual beliefs, on the other hand, then those are deeply compatible with developing Skill 15. For you, Higher Power might be God, Spirit, Source, or Creator. It might be Kabbalah's Ein Sof, it could be YHWH, Allah, the Tao, the Goddess, Jesus, Brahman, or the OverSoul. Or perhaps you prefer not to give it a name, understanding it to be the unknowable source of all that is, which in the East they call the Ground of Pure Being or Emptiness.

An important part of sustaining faith is the willingness to share your whole self with that power—however you choose to define it—including your anger, your despair, your confusion, and your fear. If you think of this as an interior dialogue between your wounded self and your Higher Self, it can help. Are you willing to allow your highest nature to absorb and hold the pain, doubts, and fears of the wounded self? If you only want to share the best parts of yourself with your Higher Power or high-est nature, feeling unworthy when you are not at your best, you will with-draw from this relationship any time you feel negative emotions. This deprives you of sustenance when you need it most.

I heard a minister say once, "It's okay to get mad at God. She can handle it." He was of course making a play on our expectations around the "gender" of God. But more importantly he was pointing out that withholding is withholding. Just as I need to let my spouse know when I am upset—or risk a slow degradation of our relationship—it is okay to be angry with your Higher Power. Whatever is large enough to be the source of all life is too large to be upset by your anger. When my daughter would get angry with me—even as a limited human I could see that my job was to allow her to have her emotions, not to invali-date them. Once her feelings were expressed we could work things through. Why would I expect less from a loving Higher Power in under-standing my upset?

Another important part of sustaining faith is being able to see even the most difficult moments in life with gratitude, knowing that howev-er challenging the moment is, this too could lead to benefit. You may not be able to see any possible gifts in the troubles you are experi-encing, especially while you are in the midst of them, but you can reflect back on exceptionally difficult times in your life and see the unexpected gifts that came out of them. This can encourage you to surrender to what you cannot control and sustain your faith through the difficulties. As I have grown older and lived through more chal-lenges, I am less afraid of the hard times. Even people who have lived through terrible situations often say that while they would not wish those circumstances on anyone else, they would not want to undo them, because those challenges and even great suffering have made them better people today. That is a powerful reframing—it does not deny the reality of suffering but sees the gift in it as well. We will talk more in Chapter 11 about using reframing techniques to help you find forgiveness and gratitude.

If you are going through a difficult time it can help enormously to put it in context. Try to think about suffering not just from your personal sub-jective perspective but from a more philosophical viewpoint. The

Buddha described life as *dukkha,* which is a hard word to translate. It essentially means that life is suffering—it is difficult and challenging. You don't have to be a Buddhist to appreciate the wisdom of this ancient mystical tradition. Buddhism's Four Noble Truths tell us that life contains suffering, that unnecessary suffering is caused by our attachment to how things "should be," that there is a route out of suffering, and that route in the Buddhist tradition is called the Eightfold Path.

Buddhists, and most of us, will acknowledge that there is some suffering that is not self-created, such as the suffering caused by death, illness, injury, loss, and the actions of others. But much of our suffering *is* self-created. We engage in self-pity and rail against God, life, the universe—which is fine and valuable up to a point—but then we don't let it go. Some of us live as though the only way we will "forgive" life is for life to undo the harm. Bring our child or our spouse or our friend back to life. Undo the tragedy of September 11, 2001. Make our spouse or our parent love us the way we want them to.

Learning to be realistic about the nature of things is part of the spiritual journey. Aging happens. People die—*I* will die. Things change. Even our Sun is not permanent—one day it will go super-nova and explode and that will be it for our little solar system. We benefit from a bigger viewpoint. I often ask myself how my particular suffering looks from the point of view of Spirit or from the perspective of the whole evolving cosmos. To temporarily experiment with these perspectives requires me to step out of and above my own problems. Once again, this is not about denying the reality or significance of my suffering and its causes, but it can help to develop resilience and to cultivate the ability to persevere and adapt when things go "wrong."

A final note on Sustaining Faith: a sense of meaning is critical to this skill. If we are to make it through the hard times without resorting to medications, denial, or addictions, we must have a "why" to live for, something beyond our own survival. Existential pain is real. We fear death, we fear suffering, and some of us fear living. We worry that it may all be meaningless. Spiritually intelligent people don't avoid this pain; they confront it and find a deeper source of meaning and purpose for living. Blind faith or hope is not enough. You must put your beliefs into daily practice in order to reap the benefits during difficult times.

Mental, emotional, physical, and spiritual discipline plays a big role in creating your state of mind—it gives rise to hopeful states that allow you to get through the days when it's all you can do to put one foot in front of the other. When we suffer we often feel despair, and this too often leads to a passive, victimized posture. Taking positive action builds up the opposites of despair—faith, hope, love—all choices we can make and spiritual muscles we can build. You will never be able to avoid all suffering as long as you exist in a human form, but developing SQ can help you to avoid the kinds of suffering that are, indeed, avoidable, and face those that are not.

Skill 16: Seeking Guidance from Higher Self

Skill 16, Seeking Guidance from Higher Self, is about developing easier access to the wisdom of the best part of you. Have you ever noticed that sometimes you just *know* what the right thing to do is, without knowing how you know? Or perhaps you have experienced moments of intuition, unexpected signals from your body, your thoughts, your feelings, or even your dreams, that have helped you make an important choice or given you much-needed direction. These are all ways that spirit, or your own Higher Self, communicates with you. We tend to be so locked into our narrow ways of thinking and our fixed perspectives on the world that we don't hear the voice of our Higher Self, so it has to find these entry points—cracks in our consciousness where it can slip through and make its wisdom available to us. In SQ we seek to develop our openness to intuition and our sensitivity to its messages. The more we practice this skill, the more accurate we find our intuitions to be.

In my own life I find that it is helpful to remember the injunction from Jesus: "Seek and ye shall find" or "Ask and you shall receive." I have a tendency to over-depend on my intellect for solving problems. Failing that, I prefer depending on my gut instinct. What I don't like doing—or better said, what my ego self does not like doing—is *waiting* to solve problems. My ego voice resists standing in uncertainty or "not knowing." Yet there are some problems that need more than my small self can bring to the table. Sometimes the questions are really big.

When I was about twelve years into my career at Exxon, I knew that I was not going to be there until retirement. I could feel the "divine discontent" stirring, nudging me to do something else. But I didn't know what that "something" was. I read books about purpose and thought about it a lot but I wasn't sure what was next. Finally, I realized it was time to turn it over to God. So I prayed and affirmed that a right and perfect next path would reveal itself. I prayed for two years before I got an answer.

I was away on a retreat when the answer hit me. I had just arrived and was sitting in an old prayer chapel. I stilled my mind and pointed my thoughts toward the Divine. Suddenly, I felt a thought arrive in my head. I heard it and felt it simultaneously. The idea was this: "Jesus with a job; Buddha with a briefcase." Wow! I was stunned. It summed up so many things for me. I had been trying to find a way to apply my spirituality at work. I was interested in Buddhism (but had not made time to study it yet). I hadn't really thought about what Jesus would do in a corporate job—but why not? So many rich ideas came flooding in. I knew in that moment that this was a pointer to my next career.

Two days later, sitting in the new prayer chapel during silent meditation, I saw in my mind a newspaper column titled "Spirit at Work." I said "Thank you!" to God/Spirit and my Higher Self/intuitive self for accessing such a brilliant idea. It named my pain and my path. How could I bring Spiritual Intelligence to the workplace? After that moment of insight, it took me five years of preparation (studying, as well as financial and emotional preparation) to leave Exxon and launch my new career. But the clarity of that guidance was profound and life-altering. And it all began with asking. So I recommend to my clients to get quiet and ask their Higher Self or Higher Power for guidance. And then listen patiently and carefully.

Quiz: Consider Your development of Quadrant 3 Skills:

For each question, decide if your current skill development is low (L), medium (M), or high (H). While this is not a validated self-assessment, it may give you some idea of your highest priorities for personal growth. (To take the full SQ21, a carefully created, researched, and validated assessment, go to www.deepchange.com.)

Skill	Question to guide you	L	M	H
12. Commitment to Spiritual Growth	I am willing to learn about spiritual topics from many sources. I commit time and energy to my own spiritual growth.			
13. Keeping Higher Self in Charge	I am able to shift intentionally from listening to the voice of my ego to listening to my Higher Self. My Higher Self voice is clear and is the primary voice I hear.			
14. Living Your Purpose and Values	My purpose and values are aligned with my Higher Self. My actions, decisions, and goals are aligned with my higher purpose and values.			
15. Sustaining Faith	I trust that there is a wise and loving nature to Life/the universe/all that is. I maintain an attitude of gratitude even when faced with difficulties.			
16. Seeking Guidance from Higher Self	I actively seek guidance from sources beyond my own logic or ego. This includes seeking the wisdom of people I respect, of great teachers/writings, and from my Higher Self or Higher Power.			

SEVEN

Social Mastery & Spiritual Presence
(Skills 17 to 21)

"Love is to the soul what food is to the body. Love is a noble act that serves others, offering respect, openness, trust, and loyalty. The more we love, the more we lose the ego-part of ourselves, and yet, in doing so, we don't become less in any way, but instead, one with those we love."

—Lance Secretan, *The Spark, the Flame, and the Torch*

This quadrant is in many ways the most complex, because the skills it contains build on the skills developed in previous quadrants. The skills that relate to social mastery and spiritual presence are in a sense the natural result of developing the self-awareness, universal awareness, and self-mastery. Skills in the fourth quadrant are accumulating all of the benefits of Quadrants 1, 2, and 3, which is why I sometimes refer to Quadrant 4 as an "outcome quadrant." While each of these skills is a specific piece of the Spiritual Intelligence puzzle, each of these also contains much of the whole. This is "advanced SQ" where you begin to put all the pieces together.

A useful analogy might be when one is learning a new physical discipline, like swimming, for example. When you watch a skilled swimmer he or she seems to move effortlessly through the water in one fluid motion. Many of us learned to do this when we were too young to even remember much of the process. But underlying that fluidity are a number of very specific movements, as a friend of mine recently discovered when she decided to learn to swim freestyle, a skill she never learned as a child. Her coach taught her using a method that began with simple drills, each designed to focus on one specific element of the stroke:

the position of the body in the water, the kicking motion, the angle at which the hand enters the water, the breathing, and the body rotation. She learned each of these movements one at a time through repetitive drills, and then once she was comfortable with the drills, her coach showed her how to connect all the pieces into a fluid freestyle stroke. The skills in Quadrants 1, 2, and 3 could be compared to those drills—each an essential element of the stroke.

When you get to Quadrant 4, you have to practice and develop your ability to put all the elements together into one fluid integrated motion so that you can move smoothly and effectively through the water. The skills we discuss in this chapter capture the essence of Spiritual Intelligence: The way you behave, and the impact you have on others. Are you a calming presence for those around you? Can you keep your heart open? Are you able to act from compassion? Are you able to act from wisdom? Are you a powerful leader and change agent by virtue of your inner strength and humility?

Quadrant 4: Social Mastery/Spiritual Presence

Skill 17. Being a Wise and Effective Teacher/Mentor of Spiritual Principles

Skill 18. Being a Wise and Effective Leader/Change Agent

Skill 19. Making Compassionate and Wise decisions

Skill 20. Being a Calming, Healing Presence

Skill 21. Being Aligned with the Ebb and Flow of Life

Skill 17: Being a Wise and Effective Teacher/Mentor of Spiritual Principles

Skill 17 is about being a wise and effective teacher of spiritual principles or spiritual laws. Some people wonder why this skill is relevant—perhaps they are not interested in being a teacher, and only want to apply the principles of SQ to their own life. But as I understand it, teaching is much more than standing on a podium giving a lecture. In a sense we are all always teaching by how we show up, how we behave. So you may not see yourself as a teacher, but as long as you are a human being who is interacting with other human beings this skill is relevant to you.

When it comes to teaching others, we can do so for many different motives. This is one way that I look at the progressive development of Skill 17—as a movement from lower motives to higher motives. The lower motives, for example, might be that you teach others out of a need to control how they think and behave. Now, this is not always a bad thing. For example, in a culture that is beset by lawlessness and tribal warfare and violence, sometimes the healthiest thing that can happen is for a religious institution to arise and teach people how to see beyond their ethnic differences, control their more primal urges, and behave in accordance with some basic moral precepts. But when we talk about spiritual intelligence we are moving to a higher level than that kind of "law and order" spirituality.

Pushing and controlling people doesn't generally work—it merely activates the other person's ego. If you have raised children you realize the limits of authoritarian methods. Becoming a magnetic attractor is much more effective when working with spiritual principles. This approach taps the Higher Self of the other person and they move towards what is highest and best for them. Effective teachers teach because they love the subject (in this case spiritual principles or spiritual intelligence) and they teach by being a positive role model. Our favorite teachers activate the "inner learner" in us—they fire our curiosity and interest so that we are then energized to learn more.

The poet Kahlil Gibran wrote, "The teacher who is indeed wise does not bid you to enter the house of his wisdom but rather leads you to the threshold of your mind." At the highest level of skill attainment you can teach by demonstrating—being—the change you (and possibly others) desire to experience in themselves and in the world around them. This does not require you to be perfect, because nobody is perfect; it means that you have integrity and you are consistent. What you teach others by words and how you behave (deeds) are the same. You walk your talk. You are peaceful, compassionate, and wise in times of stress, and your behavior during these times allows you to become a role model for others.

Skill 18: Being a Wise and Effective Leader/Change Agent

Skill 18 is about being a wise and effective leader or change agent. What does it mean to be a change agent? A change agent is someone who helps other people, groups, and organizations navigate through changes in a way that results in good solutions, faster implementation of change, and less stress and grieving. This term is used a lot in business and organizational settings, but it is not limited to those settings. Even if you are not involved in business leadership or organizational change you are undoubtedly in many other situations where you have the opportunity to be a catalyst for growth. We are all potentially social change agents. And if you are reading this book and consciously engaging with the development of your own spiritual intelligence, you are likely someone who wants to put what you learn into action for the benefit of the larger whole.

The ability to be a change agent becomes critical the moment we get involved in any kind of group or organization. If you're involved with a group in order to make a difference in the world, from the local parent-teachers association to the United Nations, you are invested in the change process. So while the language around this skill and some of the resources around this skill are more business focused, this skill applies to anybody working in any arena—politics and government, nonprofits, education, religion or business—who wants to make a difference in the world.

What's involved in being a wise and effective leader and change agent? This skill encompasses what it means to be a leader whether or not you hold that title. At a minimum, there are four key requirements for this skill: understanding all the parties; seeking win-win solutions; honoring the natural process; and ego-less (or Higher Self) participation.

The first is understanding the issues, concerns, and needs of all parties. Each of us who wants to be a change agent needs to make the effort to deeply understand the multidimensional complexity of the groups and individuals we are dealing with. This depends on the skills we have already discussed relating to understanding your own worldview and the worldviews of others. At the most basic levels this skill shows up as the ability to simply see and name the pain and suffering of all the parties involved in a change situation and to create trusting relationships with all parties. As the skill develops you feel compassion for all points of view, even those you don't agree with, and you can behave compassionately even if you don't think (from within your worldview) that someone else's suffering or grieving makes sense.

Creating effective change in the world also requires holding out for the win-win. In his book, *The 7 Habits of Highly Effective People*, Stephen Covey talks about holding to the principle of "win-win or no deal." Whenever possible, avoid the unhappy compromise. There are times when that's the best you can get. But whenever you can, push for a higher solution, one in which no one feels disgruntled or defeated and everybody feels excited about the change-process that they are engaged in and the future that they are trying to create together. This involves a willingness to resist the temptation to jump to a quick solution. Often we're so anxious to get a problem handled or an uncomfortable situation resolved that we jump to the first solution that presents itself before we've thought it through and before we've dug into the root cause of what's going on with the particular problem. As we develop our skill as a change agent we are able to avoid getting trapped into just solving the surface problem and learn to look, instead, for the root cause. At this level you also face some challenges: Are you willing to support and work towards the course of action the team decided on even if you think it is incorrect? Sometimes this is the most spiritually intelligent response; you sacrifice your own personal opinions in order to move the whole forward toward a higher win-win solution.

Finding a win-win is not always easy, but it is possible, even in situations that seem irretrievably polarized. I heard a story once about a group of antiabortion activists and a group of pro-life activists getting together in an attempt to find something they could agree on. Eventually, someone said: "What we all want is to have a world where there is no unwanted child." And that touched everybody's heart. They found a win-win. Of course the means by which those two groups would seek to reach that goal would require another debate altogether. But by establishing their common aim they started from a shared goal, and inside that container opened up the possibility of a win-win (if not today, hopefully someday).

Another key requirement is honoring the natural process. This takes patience. It's understandable to get frustrated when we can see how the world would be so much better if only we could get this, that, or the other thing to change. We can get overly aggressive and have unreasonable expectations about how fast human beings or societies can actually change. This leads not only to being less effective as change agents or leaders (we can create backlash) but also to being less happy as individuals. So having a realistic understanding of process is important.

Look around you: It takes a while for seeds planted to become ears of corn, and you can't speed up that process beyond its natural limits. Similarly, it takes people a while to come to terms with the changes that are occurring around them, to grieve for what they have to give up and to embrace what is coming as a potentially good thing. An effective change agent, a good leader, understands that one must work with the natural process. Things take the time they take and only so much can be done to accelerate that.

The last of the four requirements is egoless (or Higher Self) participation. "Egoless" doesn't necessarily mean that you have eradicated your ego altogether. In fact, if your ego is mature it can be quite an ally. What it means is that your immature ego—that contracted, self-righteous inner voice, that fear-based, angry self—is not interfering with or undermining your ability to be an effective leader and change agent. Sometimes people ask me, "Does this mean I can never be angry?" And I say, "no." Anger can be a very appropriate emotion where there is social injustice or something happening that is clearly wrong . That kind of anger comes from an expansive, open heart and a care for other people and for justice. It is very different from the kind of anger that comes from your ego feeling threatened. That kind of ego-driven anger is rarely helpful, effective, or conducive to change.

Being a wise and effective leader and change agent is a particularly complex and multidimensional skill that depends on many of the skills developed in the previous quadrants. You need to develop your awareness of self and world and master your own self to a significant degree to be in a position to embrace the demands of this kind of role and skillfully navigate the challenges it inevitably presents.

The highest test of a change agent or leader may be what he or she does when an initiative fails. Can you walk away from a failed change initiative with no loss of faith in life or other people? If a change initiative fails, do you blame others or the organization or the universe, or would you simply seek to learn how you can be a better change agent next time? This is very important in organizational change and even more so if you're dealing with social change. If you're trying to change a social issue such as discrimination or racism, it doesn't take much to get discouraged. It's only human to feel discouraged from time to time—what matters is how long you stay there. A wise and effective change agent sees a failure as an opportunity to learn how to do better in the future.

Skill 19: Making Compassionate and Wise Decisions

In Skill 19, Making Compassionate and Wise Decisions, we are again putting together many of the preceding skills. In fact, Skill 19 is an especially good example of "the complete stroke," to return to my swimming analogy, because it embodies the definition of spiritual intelligence. We have defined spiritual intelligence as the ability to behave from wisdom and compassion while maintaining inner and outer peace regardless of the situation. This skill encompasses a big piece of that definition.

The general goal of Skill 19 is Higher Self or spirit-based decisions. And remember: not making a decision IS a decision. We all make decisions all the time: the question is which part of our self is driving these decisions. I have found that the ability to make decisions from your Higher Self comes down to three things:

1. **Listen to the ego but do not be ruled by it.** The ego is an important part of us. As we mature the ego, we no longer identify with being the ego and it no longer dominates. It is in service to the Higher Self and provides important navigational advice for the world.

2. **ASK to see things with Love's eyes.** Remember to pause and ask— ask your Higher Self, ask your Higher Power—to see things with the broadest possible amount of wisdom and compassion. The way I like to phrase it is "to see things with the eyes of love." Some people like to ask, "What would Jesus do?" or, "How would Jesus see this?" It's as if you are trying to take a God's eye view. If you are not comfortable with the word God, you can pick an example of someone who inspires you. Ask "How might Gandhi see this?" The very fact that you can take that perspective connects you to your Higher Self, allowing you to relax the contracted part of yourself and intentionally call forward your Higher Self in order to see with the greatest amount of wisdom and compassion.

3. **Act from wisdom and compassion.** From that expanded perspective you can take action that is aligned with the viewpoint of your Higher Self— spiritually intelligent action that expresses wisdom and compassion.

As we break down this skill into these component parts you can see how it relies on many of the preceding skills, particularly Skill 5, the awareness of ego self and Higher Self; Skill 13, the ability to keep your Higher Self in charge; Skill 7, awareness of the worldviews of other people; Skill 9, the awareness of the limitations and power of human perception; and of course, Skill 16, seeking guidance from Higher Self or spirit or source.

Since this skill is so central to SQ, let's use it as an in-depth example of the five developmental levels, as listed in the table below:

1	I am able to make decisions that are compassionate toward myself. I am able to maintain a clear intention to develop and grow in SQ, while simultaneously not berating myself for not yet being "perfectly enlightened."
2	I am able to be compassionate toward children, spouses, relatives, and friends who are not working on their own growth in a manner or speed I might wish they were. I am able to let these significant people in my life grow as they will, knowing that I don't really know what is highest and best for every person.
3	I am able to be compassionate toward those who feel they are my enemy or who act to harm me. I set healthy boundaries around behaviors but don't hate the person who is acting out. I use power wisely, carefully—and with loving intent.
4	Universal and Higher Self awareness is so strong that my decision-making process always factors in the pain and suffering of other beings. Yet I am not paralyzed by this awareness. I take balanced actions that honor all beings.
5	Universal awareness and strong connection with Higher Self means that my inner guidance is strongly and clearly felt. With steady self-mastery, my inner guidance is translated into wise and compassionate action, which seems to flow through me from Source or Life or my Higher Power as I understand it.

At Level 1, the most basic level, Skill 19 shows up as compassion towards yourself: **I am able to make decisions that are compassionate toward myself. I am able to maintain a clear intention to develop and grow in SQ while simultaneously not berating myself for not yet "being perfectly enlightened."** This level addresses a common trap that often catches very well-intentioned people—they want to grow, they want to be good people, and then they beat themselves up when they make mistakes or unwise decisions. There's nothing wrong with having a healthy critic voice to let you know when you are out of alignment. But we don't want a hyperactive, unreasonable, perfectionist critic voice, and many of us do have one of those. Some of the most beautiful people I've met will score a 0 on this particular skill because they hold themselves to unreasonable standards. If we cannot forgive our own imperfections and have compassion towards our own mistakes we will not be fully capable of forgiving others. So the first step in developing this skill is to have compassion for yourself—including the fact that you have an ego self.

As you develop to Level 2 your compassion and wisdom turns toward others: **I am able to be compassionate toward children, spouses, relatives, and friends who are not working on their own growth in a manner or speed I might wish they were. I am able to let these significant people in my life grow as they will, knowing that I don't really know what is highest and best for every person.** As you engage with this skill you need to honestly ask yourself: Do I think that I know the best spiritual path for the significant others in my life? If so, you may not be acting in very compassionate ways toward them. Built into this skill is a belief that the spiritually intelligent approach is to let people find their own paths.

We can be there for the people we love, we can offer guidance and encouragement, but we cannot dictate. There are two reasons for this. First, I believe that I cannot know for sure what is the best spiritual path for any other person. Second, even if I am correct and I "manage" the other person's spiritual growth for them I am only creating a dependency, not helping them. There is a need for each of us to own what we learn. As with discovering our personal values, if we accept those of our family without any inquiry into those values, we won't be able to stand strong in our values-based choices during hard times. But if we wrestle with them, try other things, and then come back to some of those values by our own choosing, they then represent the deep commitment we have made and they serve us well.

No one else can build my spiritual muscle for me (see more on this topic in Chapter 8). We each have to do our own spiritual weightlifting. I think about the mistakes I have made in my life and what I have learned from them. Sometimes our loved ones need to be just as free. Free to walk away from values or spiritual practices we deeply believe in. Free to make mistakes. And we need to humbly acknowledge that what looks like a mistake to us may be perfect for them. We need to be willing to trust in the greater good and the evolutionary impulse or developmental trajectory. Short of life-threatening situations, it is usually best to allow other adults to make their own decisions. I think of it as letting God or the universe be in charge of that other person. I try to relax and trust that Spirit or God is working through them in the way that it needs to and to remember that I am not all-knowing.

Level 3 is more challenging. It states: **I am able to be compassionate toward those who feel they are my enemy or who act to harm me. I set healthy boundaries around behaviors but don't hate the person who is acting out. I use power wisely, carefully—and with loving intent.** Hopefully this will be a rare occurrence, but there are times in all of our lives when other people are angry and act out with intention to create pain for us. Can you be compassionate towards those people? They might be people in your immediate circle or people who threaten your country, like terrorists. Can you, at least at times and hopefully consistently, have compassion towards those who believe they are your enemy and/or consciously act to harm you? To reach this level you need be able to put yourself in the shoes of any other person on the planet, which takes us back to Skill 7: Understanding the Worldviews of Others.

It's important to understand that this kind of deep compassion does not mean you necessarily want to be friends with those people or that you condone the actions they might take. Part of this level of skill development is the ability to set appropriate, healthy boundaries, but to do so without falling into the ego-game of hating the other individual. This, as we discussed when we talked about forgiveness, can end up hurting you more than it hurts the other person. Being spiritual does not require you to be a wimp. Inspired by my own Christian tradition, I often think of Jesus setting boundaries in the temple by throwing out the moneychangers. It was clear that he operated from great power and strength but he was operating from power wisely, carefully, and with loving intention, which is the final element of this level of development. I find that people who have difficulty with boundaries often have trouble using their power effectively. As you develop compassion, you may also need to reclaim your ability to say "no" and really mean "no." Compassion does not mean accepting abuse from others.

At Level 4 this skill has become a natural response rather than something you have to consciously work on: **Universal and Higher Self awareness is so strong that my decision-making process always factors in the pain and suffering of other beings. Yet I am not paralyzed by this awareness. I take balanced actions that honor all beings.** This level depends on all of the Universal Awareness skills of Quadrant 2, as well as the foundational ego self/Higher Self awareness of Skill 5. The voice of my Higher Self is easily in touch with the pain and suffering of other beings, so once you learn to make that shift you will naturally feel these things and they will influence your decisions. There are some people who have developed this sensitivity, but may have become so concerned about protecting everyone involved that they become paralyzed in the decision-making process. This, again, is a developmental trap that can happen as we expand our empathy and sensitivity. If we are not careful to balance our compassion with wisdom we can get stuck in a position that is not spiritually intelligent. That desire to not want to create harm for anyone is a beautiful thing, but if you become so paralyzed that you cannot act, you end up creating pain by virtue of not being able to make a choice. Spiritual Intelligence requires that you balance this polarity. You need to be able to pause and consider the impact you're having on others, but you can't pause and consider for so long that you fail to act. Appropriately balanced between action and reflection, you will make appropriate decisions.

At Level 5 the attainment of this skill has become such a natural expression of who you are that wise and compassionate actions flow like the swimmer gliding gracefully through the water: **Universal awareness and strong connection with Higher Self means that my inner guidance is strongly and clearly felt. With steady self-mastery, my inner guidance is translated into wise and compassionate action, which seems to flow *through* me from Source or Life or my Higher Power as I understand it.** At higher stages of spiritual development many developmental psychologists agree that there tends to be an increasing absence of a selfish-self or small-self. People who are highly spiritually developed often report a feeling of being guided by something larger. At this level of development the ego is so mature and so clearly in service to Higher Self that this inner guidance feels fairly automatic. In the previous skill development we aligned ourselves with this guidance through careful practice, like repeating those drills in the pool over and over again to make our stroke as effective as possible. But now we reap the benefit of all that hard work as it feels more and more effortless. We have built new well-traveled neural pathways, and the immature ego-based pathways have gotten thinner (or been "pruned," as neuroscientists might say). That's not to say that we don't have to keep our intention focused and be alert to deliver compassionate and wise behaviors, but it has become less of a struggle to do so.

Some people object to the word "effortless," but nevertheless, it's important to use it when referring to this level of development, and it shows up in the assessment questions used to measure this skill. At Level 5 we are trying to describe the ideal. We could call Level 5 "the saintly level" for each skill. Not all of us will reach this level in this lifetime, but it is healthy to aspire to it. A saintly attainment would be one in which the ego self, or the immature ego, is so out of the way that pure transmission from source to Higher Self to action no longer requires mediation by a whole lot of internal argument and effort. The effortlessness, then, is an ideal state. To reach Level 5 in Skill 19—which in some sense is the ultimate skill since it is so closely related to the definition of SQ—one would have to be a spiritually intelligent exemplar. That's the reason the bar is set so high.

Skill 20: Being a Calming, Healing Presence

Skill 20 focuses on your ability to be a calming and healing presence. In a sense this relates to the second half of the SQ definition just as skill 19 related to the first half. Skill 20 is about your inner and outer equanimity or peace and the effect it has on others. Again, this skill is an outcome of many of the skills we have previously discussed. It is related to Higher Self or Spirit being more noticeably in charge of our lives. At the most basic level this skill may show up in the way others relate to you—people no longer try to engage you in gossip or victim stories, for example. If your Higher Self is consistently in charge people know instinctively that you're not receptive to the ego's drama.

As you develop this skill, you will notice more ways in which your presence has a calming effect on others. A wonderful illustration of this is found in Daniel Goleman's *Destructive Emotions,* where he describes some research that was done with a Tibetan Buddhist monk who had been heavily trained in compassion meditation. The researchers found that when they brought this monk together with very angry and argumentative person, the angry person would find it almost impossible to sustain their upset and argumentativeness in the face of the monk's calm conversation and lack of ego reactivity.[40] As your SQ develops you may notice that you find yourself less involved in argument or conflict. Angry people seem to run out of steam in your presence. I think of it this way: my ego is not reacting to theirs. The vicious cycle of my ego activation feeding their ego activation that then further feeds my activation is interrupted. As you progress still further, your inner and outer calm will lead to decisions and actions feeling effortlessly effective. Even today, after years of working on this, I am sometimes startled by how things can "happen on their own." I also notice this skill affects my level of energy. My energy level becomes steadier when I am in a calm and centered place. This matters, because with a steady energy level we become capable of joyful, sustainable service in which we don't get burned out. Egoic drama, tension, and conflict drains energy. When we are no longer engaging in all that, not only do we feel more energetic, but other people may report that they feel revitalized and energized in our presence. As we get focused on higher purpose and our Higher Self is present, the space between us and other people clears up because we are no longer polluting that space with ego.

Being calm and centered requires releasing our attachment to certain outcomes and our need to be in charge of situations and people. This relates to having faith in the universe and in Life. It also relates to humility. This skill requires that we let go of the "doing" and are able to just *be*. We are trained to be "human doings" and this is valuable—rapid action is sometimes necessary. But there are times when the most spiritually intelligent response is to be a "human being"—to be calmly, fully, and lovingly present to the people and situations. When we want to activate Skill 20 we release our need to act, to be the boss, to be in charge, to tell people what to do, or to force specific outcomes. When action is needed we can act from a calm center.

At the highest level of this skill you and I become beacons for the Higher Selves of others. People who attain this degree of SQ seem to radiate love and non-judgment, and because of that other people near them are better able to access their Higher Selves. Win-win solutions to problems may spontaneously become apparent and others may say they feel profoundly peaceful in the presence of the person demonstrating mastery of this skill.

Skill 21: Being Aligned with the Ebb and Flow of Life

The last of the 21 Skills is about being aligned with the ebb and flow of life. Life is a process, an unpredictable and ever-changing stream. If you try to steer a perfectly straight course against the current of the stream you are likely to face continuing frustration as you run into rocks, get spun around by unexpected eddies, and struggle against the momentum of the water. Spiritually intelligent people understand this and learn to move with the flow of the life-process to draw on inner intuition, a sensitivity to their own bodies, and an awareness of the world around them to help them navigate. This can show up as an ability to sense when the timing is right for to act on something or to discern that obstacles that may arise in your path can have multiple meanings, none of which are predetermined. As you develop this skill you recognize the difference between the blessings and distractions that appear in your path, and you may find that the right people and resources naturally appear when you need them. Synchronicities occur more frequently as you line up with the direction that the evolutionary impulse or direction of life and growth is flowing.

Body awareness is an important part of this skill. This is why it is one of the intersection points between SQ and PQ. To be aligned with the ebb and flow of life you need to be aligned with the energy flows in your own body. Our bodies are part of this material universe, and the universe is filled with energy flows, so tuning in to your body is a way of tuning in to the universe. As you align with the ebb and flow of life you can align with this energy. You can align with the natural/social/cultural process that you are participating in and understand how, as the Taoists tell us, a tiny touch can guide the world. You learn to notice subtle changes in your energy level. You need to interpret what your body is telling you: Are you tired because you forgot to eat and your blood sugar is low? Or are you picking up on the energy in the room? Learning to read your own body signals helps you stay in touch with the natural ebbs and flows. Like a Geiger counter that picks up radiation, your body is a fantastic guide to what is going on in the larger milieu in which you are embedded, and it can help you develop "natural timing"—an intuitive sense of when to push ahead and when to pause.

Taoism is a wonderful resource for understanding this skill. The very concept of the Tao encompasses this sense of the ebb and flow of life in all its mystery and wholeness. There are many wonderful, mystical sayings in Taoism, such as "The master does nothing and leaves nothing undone." It conveys the idea that a tiny touch applied at the exact right moment can create perfect action and yet to an outside observer it may appear that the master did nothing. The master accomplishes great things through these tiny touches. Guided by natural timing and aligned with the energy flows, you can apply the right level of touch at the right time and be far more effective.

At the highest level of this skill, you live joyfully in the eternal present moment. Who you are and what you do is an effortless dance. When spiritual intelligence is flowering at this level, you may sense that instead of you being the one who is doing something, it's the universe that is doing something through you, and it is a joyful, beautiful dance.

The Payoff

In conclusion, we can say that the skills of Quadrant 4—the skills of social mastery and spiritual presence—are where your work in the previous quadrants "pays off." As we look at the spiritual exemplars you might hold up as heroes or role models for yourself, you can probably see that they embody some of these skills. A good question to ask yourself is: Are there any of these skills that I *would not* want to have in your own personal toolkit or see demonstrated in your family, nation, or workplace? For me the answer is "no." I want all of these and I want them in abundance for myself and for my world. So if we want these, what are we waiting for? By breaking SQ into pieces we now have a way we can start developing it.

Quiz: Consider Your Development of Quadrant 4 Skills:

For each description decide if your current skill development is low (L), medium (M), or high (H). While this is not a validated self-assessment, it may give you some idea of your highest priorities for personal growth. (To take the full SQ21, a carefully created, researched and validated assessment, go to www.deepchange.com.)

Skill	Question to guide you	L	M	H
17. Being a Wise and Effective Teacher/Mentor of Spiritual Principles	I enjoy teaching about spiritual principles. I do that through walking my talk and awakening the learner in other people.			
18. Being a Wise and Effective Leader/Change Agent	I can see and feel the perspectives of all the parties involved in a change. I am able to release my need to control or to have things my way.			
19. Making Compassionate and Wise Decisions	I am compassionate toward my own mistakes as well as those made by others. I know how to set boundaries when I need to do so.			
20. Being a Calming, Healing Presence	Other people feel calmer in my presence.			
21. Being Aligned with the Ebb and Flow of Life	I instinctively know what is trying to come into form, and I can apply the right amount of action when it is needed to assist the process.			

PART THREE

Developing Your Spiritual Intelligence

EIGHT

Spiritual Weightlifting

*"We are what we repeatedly do.
Excellence, then, is not an act, but a habit."*

—Will Durant, *The Story of Philosophy*

H aving come this far, you should now have a good understanding of the rich and complex skill-set that makes up what I call Spiritual Intelligence. In the last four chapters we have examined each of the 21 Skills that my model has identified, which are measured by the SQ21. You may be starting to wonder, how do I go about developing all of these different capacities? And where should I start?

Each of these skills takes cultivation and practice, and there are many tools you can use to help you in your development—from ancient spiritual practices to cutting-edge psychological methods. While the model is complex and multidimensional, the essence of Spiritual Intelligence is quite simple: it is about shifting from ego to Higher Self. In this chapter I will share with you the basic principles for making and sustaining this shift that you can begin practicing right now. If you are interested in engaging with your own spiritual growth skill-by-skill, I recommend that you first take the SQ21 assessment. It will give you a starting point for each skill, highlight the areas that you need to focus on and suggest specific next steps. I have also included a short list of resources in the back of this book to support you in your development and further resources are available on my website. However, let's look first at the basics of how SQ development works.

Remember, Spiritual Intelligence is defined as *the ability to behave with wisdom and compassion while maintaining inner and outer peace regardless of the circumstances.* And once again, the word "behave" is critical. SQ is not about just feeling in touch with your Higher Self. That is relatively easy to accomplish when you are sitting quietly alone in prayer or meditation. SQ is about how we behave—how we actually make decisions and act—in the everyday, stressful world of interacting with other people and complex situations. Do I have enough integrity to show up in the way I claim I want to show up? Once you have identified the difference between your ego and your Higher Self, the all-important question is: Can you shift? Once you hear the voice of your Higher Self, can you make the transition from acting on ego to acting on that Higher Self? The bottom line is that if you're going to be more spiritually intelligent you need to begin to act less from your ego and more from your Higher Self.

Virtually all of the world's major faith traditions, philosophies, and psychologies encourage the development of understanding others and kindness. Many traditions perceive this "right action" and "right understanding" as being in service of something larger than the individual self—a universal principle or a Higher Power. But if you are not comfortable with that kind of language, it is not necessary to adopt it. If you understand the difference between your ego and your Higher Self you simply need to start making choices based on listening to the voice of your Higher Self and *act* upon what it is telling you. If you do this your behavior will change, sometimes quite dramatically. And it is behavior we are looking at to determine, ultimately, the level of SQ development. Interior awareness matters—but it must be translated into action. And sometimes taking the right action can contribute to the development of interior awareness. Awareness enlightens action, and then we take the action and see what happens. We learn from that action through the feelings we experience in our interior and from the reaction or result we experience on the exterior. Interior development feeds exterior behaviors, and exterior behaviors continue to feed interior development. The joy I get from my improvements motivates me to keep improving—it is a virtuous circle. So my bias is toward learning AND doing—not waiting for full enlightenment before modifying how we show up in the world.

People often ask me if this isn't an overly pragmatic approach to spiritual development. Can we really "behavior-modify" ourselves into being more spiritual people? Some feel that spirituality is not something we can develop at all. "Spiritual is what you already are," they tell us. Others say that spirituality is a matter of inner realization, a connection to Spirit, or to some form of divine inspiration. Changes in behavior naturally result if the realization is deep enough, they declare. And while I don't deny that this can be true, it is not always the case. Many people have had powerful revelations but continue to act in ways that lack integrity, care, and compassion for others. We have only to look at the painful legacy of some of the more popular spiritual teachers in the past few decades to see this. On the other hand, we can also find examples of individuals who struggled inwardly with their faith, yet continued to act in inspiring and exemplary ways.

One of the most extraordinary illustrations of this principle can be found in the private journals of Mother Teresa that recently became available, revealing that the great saint, who was such an example to millions, lived much of her life in a state of spiritual anguish because she felt that she had lost the direct connection to God that she had felt in her early life. But did this stop her from continuing her life's work? Did this make her less compassionate, less selfless, less available to those who needed her? To my knowledge, it did not. Of course, we would all prefer to feel that inner connection all the time, to hear the voice of God or our Higher Self clearly. But Mother Teresa's example of sustaining faith (Skill 15) shows that we can behave with wisdom and compassion even in times of inner challenge. And this is critical, because I don't think most of us can afford to wait until we feel perfectly developed on the inside. There are very few Ramana Maharshis or Eckhart Tolles around, so the rest of us need to stop waiting for instant enlightenment and get down to work.

Our "spiritual muscles" are much like our physical ones. If you want to develop your body you begin by accepting the fact that you are not already perfectly fit. And your desired state of fitness is unlikely to descend on you one day as you relax in a recliner. So you go to the gym and lift weights and trigger a process of development. It's not that you have to make effort every waking moment. But if you make the right effort at the right times—

applying focus, intention, and discipline to your workout—this sets in motion a growth process that continues even when you stop the activity. Muscles grow while we sleep. Physiological research has shown that when we lift weights, for example, we break down muscle tissue. Then when we stop our activities, particularly when we are resting, nature attempts to rebuild the broken layers of tissue, building them a little stronger than last time. Over a period of continuous destroying and rebuilding our muscles grow and adapt to the strain we put on them.

Neuroscientists have discovered in the last decades that the human brain is remarkably "plastic" or moldable. We are in a constant process of building new neural networks and pruning off ones we don't need any longer. When we try a new behavior we build a new neural pathway. If I snapped at Joe every time he said "hello" to me in the past, I have developed a thick neural pathway to support that habit. Initially, it's quite awkward to force my own brain down a new route and choose a new option—like smiling and saying good morning to Joe. If I do it one day and then stop, I won't build a new neural network. But if I make a practice of doing it every day for a month or two the new neural pathway becomes thicker and the habit of saying "Good morning, Joe" becomes easier. Simultaneously, the old habit and the neural pathway that supported it gets thinner and weaker. My "instinctive" reaction to Joe now defaults to "Good morning, Joe" and a smile.

What is especially fun is the way in which building one set of muscles can support other muscles and have unexpected benefits. I began a regular routine of physical training two years ago. I had undergone surgery for a herniated disc and didn't ever want to find myself in that situation dealing with that much pain again. I decided I had better get proactive about maintaining my muscles. So now, whenever I am in town I go three days a week and work out with my trainer, Mary Jean Tiernan. She is very skilled at making sure I work a lot of different muscles, including ones I didn't even know I had—at least until they were aching the next day! Yet she is also careful not to push me so hard that I injure myself. Initially, my balance, strength, and coordination were pretty pathetic. I have been working at a desk more or less since college. And once kids came along, the time for personal exercise dwindled. I walked regularly, but that was it. With aging, I was losing muscle. So I had to turn things around.

Over time, with a consistent routine of "just enough" exercise to stretch the muscles and strain them, tasks got easier. My weight levels on the machines won't threaten any of the regular "gym rats," but I feel so much stronger. Everyday tasks are easier, like moving suitcases in and out of the car and carrying groceries. My posture has improved. My clothes fit better. And people consistently tell me I look younger and stronger. And now when Mary Jean poses a new challenge at the gym like "stand on this wobbly surface and balance yourself while you do X," my core is strong enough to hold me and I can do the exercise. The whole process has become more fun and the rewards are clear.

In the same way that I was unaware of the interacting power of my stronger muscles, deliberately practicing any skill of Spiritual Intelligence can lead to more changes than just the ones that come from that particular skill. The whole effort of developing SQ is an iterative process. If you make the right effort to act differently you may become aware of parts of yourself that you could not previously perceive. You become more self-aware. You release a little bit of your previous identity, a sense of your persona. For example, you might have always thought, "I am a person with a short temper." But then you find yourself demonstrating patience. It may have required you to bite your lip, but you did it. You can now think, "I am a person who can choose to be patient." With practice, patience becomes more and more natural. You build thicker neural pathways with each repetition. Eventually, you might think, "I am a patient person." So now you have the courage to try one more new behavior. And that new behavior generates another shift in self-understanding. In addition, you see tangible benefits in your relationships—with your family, your friends, your team, and your company. You activate a "success loop" that builds momentum and motivates you to keep going. You have built a "stronger core."

This kind of "spiritual weightlifting" is definitely a pragmatic approach, but it is an appropriate way to approach every aspect of our development. This is especially true for those of us in leadership positions when behavior has direct effects on the people who look to us for guidance. In one way or another, we are all leaders and are all role models—to our children, to our employees, to people we may not even have met. When I speak about leadership I am not restricting my advice to those who have attained positions of management or authority. What I call "deep leadership" is a key human quality that each one of us should aspire to develop. Deep, authentic leadership means that we lead ourselves first. We lead ourselves to a deep inner self-awareness and an expanded awareness of the world around us. We build the multiple intelligences we need in order to be worthy of being emulated. And we do our spiritual weightlifting so that we can master ourselves and connect to and live from our highest self, guided by our highest purpose and values.

Embracing this responsibility means taking a profoundly pragmatic approach to our own transformation. After all, if we are waiting for a miraculous transformation, and in the meantime continue to act out of ego, what kind of message are we sending to those who observe us? We all must have the upper hand over less mature responses and reactions if we are to be catalysts for lasting and meaningful change in the lives of others and in the world around us. Through developing awareness and self-mastery we can take responsibility for ourselves—for our less mature tendencies and impulses as well as our highest potentials—so that our actions have the most positive effects on those around us.

Parker Palmer, a wise and eloquent author and educator, puts it beautifully: "A leader is a person who has an unusual degree of power to project on other people his or her shadow or his or her light. A leader is a person who has an unusual degree of power to create the conditions under which other people must live and move and have their being—conditions that can either be as illuminating as heaven or as shadowy as hell. A leader is a person who must take special responsibility for what's going on inside him or her self, inside his or her consciousness, lest the act of leadership create more harm than good."

When we hear the words "great leader" or "spiritual leader" we tend to think of lofty examples like Nelson Mandela or Mahatma Gandhi. And while these great figures are certainly more than worthy of that designation, I encourage people to consider that we each can be spiritual leaders too. When I first consulted with a major Houston hospital I was asked to conduct a "Spiritual Leadership" training for the leaders among the nursing staff. I began, as I did in the opening chapters of this book, by asking them to give me examples of people they admired as spiritual leaders. Besides the great nation builders and human rights activists and saints, many of them cited their own Chief Nursing Officer, Dr. Pamela Triolo. I later worked with Pamela's group at another medical center and the same thing happened. I found out the reason her staff held her in such high esteem was first and foremost her commitment to her own spiritual work, and secondly, her commitment to help other people with their development. Like someone who is committed and consistent in going to the gym, her spiritual weightlifting was paying off. The work she was doing on her own interior showed up consistently in her behavior. This made her a great listener who cared deeply about the growth of the organization and the individuals who worked there. She held a long-term perspective on what was going on and worked to serve the whole. She was a true "servant leader" and a great model for the power of "leading yourself first." And as a result, her leadership teams gave the same commitment to those who worked for them. As I shared in Chapter 3, the health system where I first met Pamela became a Fortune Top 100 employer and remains one to this date. Her leadership was a big part of that transformation.

The moral of the story is that Spiritual Intelligence, like a more muscular, fit body, is available to all of us if we are willing to work for it. The requirements are simple. Recognize that you have inside of you the voice of a smaller self (your ego) and the voice of a Higher Self. Learn to listen to the Higher Self. Then build the muscle (discipline) to act on the advice of your Higher Self. With SQ, as with weight lifting, you have to start with reasonable exercise levels and slowly build up. The next chapter includes the 9 Steps that I have found helpful in this "spiritual weight lifting" process. With consistent practice of these steps you can build the capacity to forgive, release the drama in your life, see options, and generate creative solutions. You learn to act from wisdom and compassion while maintaining a peaceful center.

NINE

Nine Steps to Shift to Higher Self

*"What saves a man is to take a step. Then another step.
It is always the same step, but you have to take it."*

—Antoine de Saint-Exupery, *Wind, Sand, and Stars*

There is an old adage that begins with a question: "How do you eat an elephant?" The answer is: "One bite at a time." One bite at a time is great advice for spiritual development, too. We may look at someone we admire—someone like Nelson Mandela, Mother Teresa, Gandhi, or Abraham Lincoln—and think, "I can't do that. I can't BE that." Yet the truth is that we can become like them. We can do it—one step at a time—one "spiritual weightlifting" exercise at a time. A methodical approach can truly pay off. That is why I eventually created a 9-step process for myself. I found it reassuring to know that when I took a little time and worked through the steps, I saw a difference right away. So, today you might find a new way of behaving with that really rude store clerk and tomorrow find a new way of behaving with your difficult coworker. Next month—maybe you will feel strong enough to find a new way to interact with a difficult family member!

What I am happy to tell you is that in many ways this does get easier with practice. What may get harder are the problems you choose to apply yourself to—like moving up to heavier weights at the gym once you have established a level of basic fitness and are familiar with the exercises. But when you work from the smaller problems in your life and go up to the larger ones, you find that "the elephant" was not nearly as large or as difficult to manage as you thought.

That being said, managing the ego should not be underestimated. It can be difficult to make the shift to one's Higher Self in the heat of the moment once the ego is provoked. But this is where it really counts. Recognizing the difference between your ego and your Higher Self *after* you yelled at your assistant for something that wasn't really her fault or after you were defensive with your husband over a simple mistake won't undo the damage. A spiritually intelligent person learns to shift in the midst of the challenging moment to prevent the ego from driving her actions. These 9 steps help you make that shift—and sustain that shift. Unlike crazy yo-yo dieting plans or short-term muscle-building, if you keep at this process you will find that you can sustain it. The happiness it brings you becomes the self-reinforcing feedback loop that keeps you on track and helps you get back on track when you suffer a momentary ego-hijack.

I realize nine steps is a lot and you may be wondering how you'll have time for this in those heated moments when it really counts—such as when you're standing in the hallway at work confronted by the co-worker who has once again taken credit for your hard work. In those moments you may need to turn to what I call the "Four Step Shortcut for Daily Use" described in the following chapter. But it is important to understand the full process, because putting all of these steps into practice is essential for your long-term development. One of the most important functions of this process is that it gets you to slow down, to create space around what are usually unconscious and habitual reactions. Imagine you are taking a moment of intensity and switching it into slow motion. The very act of doing this runs counter to the "heat of the moment." So try to practice all nine steps whenever you can.

The list below gives you an overview of the trajectory of this shift. In this chapter, we walk through the steps one by one:

Nine Steps to Shift

Step 1: **STOP**

Step 2: **BREATHE**

Step 3: **ASK for help**

Step 4: **OBSERVE yourself**

Step 5: **IDENTIFY and Embrace Ego-concerns**

Step 6: **LOOK DEEPLY for root causes of ego-concerns**

Step 7: **REFRAME the situation—see with new eyes**

Step 8: **FOCUS on something to be Grateful for**

Step 9: **CHOOSE a spiritually intelligent response**

Step 1. STOP ("insert pause here!")

The first step is the simplest but often the hardest. In the midst of a challenging moment, can you stop? Can you "insert a pause" between an event that has triggered something within you and the habituated response that is bursting to get out? It may sound like an easy thing to do, but if you have ever tried it you know that it can take enormous spiritual effort and self-awareness to create even the smallest space between reaction and response in such a moment. I'm not asking you to necessarily let go of your typical behavior—it might be a perfectly understandable and even appropriate response to the situation. But can you pause for a moment and suspend it? This step is absolutely critical because it is the only place that your Higher Self can gain power.

I use the image of a freight train as a metaphor for ego activation. When you are calm, it is as if the train is stopped in the station. Your higher brain functions (in the neocortex) are functioning nicely. IQ is online. Hopefully your Higher Self is present—at least in the background—and you are operating in a way that would be just fine if it appeared on the front page of a newspaper (or got blasted across the Internet). Then something happens. A coworker says that thing she always says in meetings that just drives you nuts. Or your dad starts to lecture you once again on your love life (or lack thereof). And the upset begins. It is as if an inner whistle blows and suddenly the "ego train" starts to pull out of the station. Biologically speaking, it is estimated that there are just six seconds between when your trigger (that hot button that others seem to find and know just how to push) activates and when you are in full limbic-system hijack. That short time is the difference between the train pulling away from the station and when it is racing down the track out of control. In full hijack we often say and do things that we regret. It is imperative that we learn to feel the first movement of that train and apply the brakes quickly. The sooner you stop the train of your ego upset, the better! So how do we do that?

Nothing can change without our intention being clearly set to break the pattern. Step 1 begins when you NOTICE the first motion of the "train." Learn to detect what you feel in your body, mind, and emotions as the ego activates in defense against a perceived threat. And as soon as you feel the first inklings of that internal motion—say "STOP!" to yourself. I actually visualize a stop sign or imagine that I am holding up my hand like a police officer in front of the train, saying "HALT!" In this simple motion, you activate the impulse control center of your brain. And this is the beginning of everything when it comes to SQ development.

Step 2. BREATHE

Once you have gained the mental upper hand by saying "STOP!" to that ego train, take four or five long, slow, deep belly breaths. A belly breath means that your belly button should push out as you inhale. Put your hand over your belly button and practice breathing so deeply your stomach pushes out into your hand. Believe it or not, slow deep breaths help to manage ego activation on a biological level. You may notice that when your ego-response is triggered, your breathing becomes rapid and shallow. This is a physiological reaction to the perceived threat in the form of your boss, sibling, or whoever has set you off. It is one of the symptoms of the activation of the limbic system, which in turn activates the sympathetic nervous system, which is designed to help you survive. Your instinctive "fight or flight" mechanisms are set in motion. This includes a rush of adrenaline and the flow of blood away from your neocortex, the seat of your higher mind-functions. This is why at such moments you are likely to do and say things that in calmer, more rational moments you would never consider. So taking long, slow belly breaths signals to your body that all is well. After all, would you be taking long slow relaxed breaths if a tiger was attacking? Doing this tells your brain and body that there is no threat present. This reactivates the parasympathetic nervous system that in turn calms the limbic system and allows your higher brain to come back online. If you do this silently, for just a few moments, you create space for your Higher Self to be heard. You will get relief on just the first breath. And by doing four or five of these, I always find that my body hormones have shifted and my Higher Self can come back into the picture.

Sometimes, to take these first two steps (STOP and BREATHE), you may find that you need to create actual space and time for yourself. Make a simple excuse and put a phone call on hold if necessary to allow yourself to stop and breathe. I learned this trick unexpectedly one day when I answered the phone at work in the office. A manager launched immediately into what felt like an attack on our procedures and a listing of how incompetent we were. I interrupted him in my most polite, professional voice and said, "Excuse me, may I put you on hold? I want to get rid of this other call so I can listen to you." He was startled and stammered out, "Uh . . . okay."

There was no other call. I put him on hold and took a long, slow deep breath and set my intention to show up to him as a good listener. It took about five or ten seconds. I got back on the call and said, "I am so sorry. Tell me how I can help you." In that time, I had calmed down and so had he. He started by saying, "Look, I know this isn't your fault, but here is the problem . . ." While he was still upset, we had a good conversation and I promised to investigate and get right back to him. I did, and I was able to create a positive customer experience for him in remediating the problem. What gave me that idea to put the call on hold? Intuition? Higher Self? I don't know, but I am so grateful for that inspiration in that moment. We both "got our brains back online" and were able to have a constructive interaction.

In a similar vein, a good friend and colleague of mine was getting feedback about her temper. She had confided in me that she had been told that she had to stop having outbursts in meetings. A few weeks later we were in a meeting together that became tense. I could feel her anger simmering and nearing boiling point, so I interrupted everyone and said, "I really need a five-minute bathroom break—would that be okay?" Now, who is going to say "no" to that? Everyone acted a little embarrassed as I moved quickly out of the meeting room in the direction of the restroom. But I didn't leave before tapping my friend lightly on the shoulder and saying, "Coming with me?" She knew what I was doing and followed me to the restroom where, once she had taken a few long deep breaths, she thanked me profusely for keeping her from saying something that would have gotten her in trouble. We talked about how to proceed. And when we returned everyone had calmed down and we had a good conversation and agreed on next steps for the project.

Don't be too embarrassed or too proud to simply ask for the time you need. No one is going to say no to putting a call on hold or going to the bathroom. You can also just ask for a few minutes or even overnight to think things over before responding to a question or a situation that is agitating you. These seemly inconsequential actions can carry the potential for huge spiritual muscle-building.

Step 3. ASK for help (from Higher Self, the Divine, or other people!)

The third step is to ask for help. You may not be a religious person who is accustomed to praying, but you don't need to believe in God to acknowledge that you need help. You can ask your own Higher Self (you may call it your intuition or inner guidance) or even envision someone you trust and respect and ask them in an internal mental dialogue (Hey, Grandma, how would you handle this?). In so doing, you create space around your habitual reaction. You practice the humility to recognize the need for change and to acknowledge that you may not have all the answers yourself—at least not in the dimensions of yourself (ego) that you habitually respond from.

If someone is available, ask a trusted human being. "Here is the situation . . ." (summarize without drama, as best you can) ". . . what would be the compassionate and wise thing to do here?" It is important that you pick someone who is committed to helping you in this spiritual weight-lifting process. Ideally, this someone is also doing this work. Sometimes when I am upset and need to release some of the ego's reactions, I set an agreement with the person—"Hey, I need to vent about this for a few minutes. Watch the clock. If I have vented for more than five minutes, cut me off." The logic for this is that any benefit you are going to get from "discharging" your upset is gained only in the first few minutes of venting. After that, you are actually activating more upset in yourself. This time limit also keeps you more focused on the facts rather than the "Can you believe it?!" and "Who does she think she is?"

kinds of comments. Whether in dialogue with a friend or with your own Higher Self, quickly move to the question, "What is the loving (compassionate and wise) thing to do in this situation? What is loving to me, to him/her, to the others involved?"

Finally, one very important addition: if you have a belief in God or a Higher Power by any name through your faith tradition or any form of spirituality, this is the step where you can insert prayer. My favorite prayer involves the word "Help!" Sometimes I just think, "Help" as its own prayer. Sometimes, I say it inside more fully: "Help me, God. Help me know what is the most loving thing to do in this situation. What can I do to create the highest and best outcome for everyone?" If faith is important to you, there is tremendous power and calming impact in using this moment for prayer. But once again, an explicitly religious or even spiritual context is not necessary. You can be an atheist and still ask your Higher Self for guidance.

Step 4. OBSERVE yourself (body, heart, mind)

Now that you have created some inner space through stopping, breathing, and asking for help, you can start to pay attention to what is going on in yourself. Once again, this may seem like a lot to do in a moment of intensity, but as you get the hang of it you can move through these steps very quickly until they eventually become a new habit. However, it is important to give yourself the space to learn how to do this.

As I mentioned in Step 2, there are easy ways to give yourself a little break from a tense moment. Of course, there are times when this won't be possible, and in those times you can use the "Shortcut" described in Chapter 11. But if you can take a few moments, follow all of the nine steps, and observe your experience, this gives you access to a deeper self-understanding and self-empowerment in the face of your own habitual responses. We want to learn to OBSERVE three dimensions of our experience: body, emotions, and thoughts.

Begin by paying attention to your body. Are you tense? Observe your muscles. Are you clenching your teeth, making a fist, going red with embarrassment, or feeling a "knot" in your stomach? Do you feel a pain in your neck or back?

Then move to your emotional state. Can you name the emotions that are arising—anxiety, fear, anger, and so on? Naming an emotion is incredibly powerful. When you bring a feeling into a WORD you have pulled yourself into your neocortex—into the language and logic centers of your brain. You can now see something as an object to look at instead of being "run by it." You have moved into the driver's seat.

Lastly, turn to your thoughts. Notice the thoughts you are having and the ways in which they are creating or amplifying your emotional state. We tend to believe that emotions "happen to us"—that they are "caused by others." You can hear this in how we speak about our emotions: "He made me so mad!" In fact, emotions are (with a few biological exceptions) caused by our interpretations of what is happening in the outside world. We interpret something as a threat, and in a split second we have a threat response. This usually happens so fast that we don't realize what's happening. Training ourselves to observe our emotions and examine the thoughts behind them brings this process into conscious awareness, into the neocortex, where we can work with them. We can change our responses and eventually with practice no longer be upset by the things that used to trigger us. This is the real power of SQ—releasing anger-triggers that no longer serve us.

To illustrate the process of observing, imagine this scenario: a coworker in a meeting points out an error in my presentation in front of my boss. I may feel the physical flush of heat in my face. I may clench my jaw. I may notice anxiety, embarrassment, and anger surging through me in emotional waves. Certain assumptions and conclusions spring up in my mind: "He must be out to get me. He wants my job. He's deliberately trying to undermine me," and so on. At this point in the process I don't judge my responses or try to suppress them—I just observe their arising with as much equanimity as I can muster. I might say to myself, "Ah, there I go—I feel it happening—I am clenching my teeth. I feel anger, embarrassment, and worry. I am interpreting this as a threat."

Step 5. IDENTIFY and Embrace Ego-concerns

In the scenario described above my ego is not entirely wrong. In fact, the ego usually has a piece of the truth, but that piece tends to be exaggerated. The purpose of the ego is to keep you safe. It doesn't care if it's being a drama queen. It would rather overreact than under-react. In the logic of the ego's fight-or-flight system, overreaction is no problem at all. But under-reacting could be fatal. So which of the ego's fears might be true in the scenario of the coworker pointing out a mistake? I like to enter fully into the perspective of the ego to see what it is afraid of and what might be true before I start discounting it.

So let's examine the ego's point of view—and allow it to go "full drama queen" in its concerns. Do not filter it, yet. Go with ego's perspective. Yes, it is possible that I may be looking like a fool in front of my boss. But that is not all my ego is worried about. It feels embarrassed in front of my coworkers. It feels competition with the guy who pointed out the mistake. It is worried about being incompetent ("How did I miss that mistake? I proofread this three times!"). In this story I might instantly (and unconsciously) conclude that this coworker is intentionally *trying* to make me look bad. I assume that he is competing with me and my loss is automatically his gain. If I ask my ego, "What are you defending me from?" or "Why are you feeling defensive?" it might answer: "I am defending you because you worked hard on this and a typo has nothing to do with the recommendation you are making. I care about this recommendation getting approved. And this idiot might be undermining us and we won't get the approval. This is not ok! And you deserve credit for your hard work. You deserve a bonus for this work. I won't let him get in the way."

Notice that I am giving my ego a chance to speak to me as a separate voice (ego) addressing me (Cindy). This is a typical voice-dialogue technique in psychology—allowing the separate voices of the self to have a conversation. I didn't know that when I began practicing this technique, but it turns out this is a powerful psychological and spiritual tool to increase self-awareness and self-development. Voice dialogue creates a separation that is helpful. I am not my ego; I *have* an ego. The more central self, "Cindy," can listen to "the voice of my ego." I can then talk back to it and say "Thank you. I know you are trying to defend us. And you are right to be worried about these things. You can relax now. I see what is going on and I will handle it. You can turn it over to me." I use an internal tone of voice that is similar to the tone I would use with a scared child: very loving, very reassuring. The short form that I use now is, "Thank you! I appreciate the warning. I've got it from here, my friend."

Treating the ego as an ally is more helpful than making an enemy of it. In the spiritual world there is a popular saying: "What we resist, persists." Fighting the ego puts it even more on the defensive and makes it more frightened, stronger, and less likely to calm down. Recognize that it is serving the whole of you, albeit in a hyperactive and drama-prone way. We can love it, appreciate it, and help it to calm down by listening to it. I have found this to be a hugely helpful way of interacting with ego. Love works better than attack.

I find this step important because I value the alarm system of the ego. It is overly dramatic and easily triggered, but it is also very valuable. There is information in the alarm. It just needs to be filtered and managed. Embrace the ego's concern as a potentially useful piece of information. Thank your ego for wanting to protect you. And then move on to Step 6.

Step 6. LOOK DEEPLY for root causes of ego concerns (Ask "Why?" 5+ times)

In Step 5 we've looked at the surface layer of the ego's fears. Step 6 looks deeper: What does the ego *really* fear? I will tip you off to the answer. There are, according to Jungian psychologists, two root fears of the ego: abandonment and death, on one hand, and overwhelm and loss of identity (another form of death) on the other.

If as children we were abandoned by our caregivers because we displeased them or they lost interest in us, we would have literally died. The human species has an incredibly long period of parent-child dependency compared to other species. This is a trade-off in terms of survival. This "prolonged childhood" enables our highly complex brains to retain plasticity, allowing for tremendous learning and adaptation, but it also renders us physically dependent on a caregiver in a way that is inherently scary.

Our other deep-rooted fear is of being overwhelmed or engulfed by another. In the movie *Psycho,* the lead male character, Norman Bates, was completely enmeshed with his mother and was crippled developmentally as a result. He had no separated self-sense. This is the other core fear of the ego. We want to be loved and protected and cared for but we don't want to be smothered. Psychological abandonment and its opposite, engulfment, are both terrifying to the ego self.

These core fears are often buried beneath lots of other "explana-tions" for what we are upset about. It takes some work to get down to the core fear and then to "come back up" to a higher perspective that releases the fear and takes the charge out of an upset. While this step might at first seem unnecessary or even silly, when I try to skip it, the upset tends to linger. So please don't skip this. Bandaging over the top of an upset is no more helpful than bandaging over the top of a fester-ing wound. We need to open the whole thing up to the light of con-sciousness. Then true insight and healing can take place.

So let's take this next step. Once you have identified the concerns of the ego, you need to dig deep to find its roots and understand why the particular situation is so highly emotionally charged. The way to do this is to keep asking your ego self, "Why are you afraid of that? What is real-ly going on?" This works best if you take on the voice of the Higher Self as the one who is asking the questions. Ask the ego as if it were anoth-er person—a young child whom you are nurturing and trying to help. I love to visualize a wise mentor from favorite stories asking the young and foolish hero some questions (think of Yoda or Obi Wan Kenobi of *Star Wars* talking to the young Luke Skywalker).

Continuing with the example I gave earlier, where the coworker point-ed out my mistake, I (the voice of my Higher Self) might begin by asking my ego: "Why are you worried about looking like a fool in front of the boss?" The first answer from the voice of my ego self (which sounds like a scared or angry youth) could be, *"What, are you dumb? Because it will affect my performance rating! I will drop down in the ratings."* Then ask again: Why are you worried about that? What is at risk? *"I'll get a smaller salary increase, a smaller bonus, I may lose promotion opportunities."* And why are you worried about that? *"At best, I won't fulfill my potential. I might have to leave the company to ever get promoted. At worst, I might lose my job if there is a layoff!"* Ask again: "Why are you worried about los-ing your job?" (At this point, you may feel like the questions have become silly. But stay with the process.) *"If I lose my job, I can't pay my bills."* Why are you worried about that? *"What, are you nuts? I'll lose my house if I can't pay the mortgage."* Why are you worried about that? *"Apart from total humiliation? I'll be homeless!!"* At a certain point, you'll quite possi-bly start to laugh as you recognize that the scenario your ego is playing out is quite ridiculous and highly unlikely to actually occur. But the important point to recognize here is: *this unlikely scenario is in fact what is driving your ego's responses.* And that is why the ego's reaction to such a petty event as someone pointing out a typo in my presentation is so emotionally charged and disproportionate to the actual threat; through the lens of your neocortex and Higher Self, you will learn to recognize this.

Remember, the ego is designed to keep you safe, and it sees a death threat in little things. It goes from minor alert to full-scale nuclear war threat level very easily. It is up to us to manage the behavior of our own limbic system by bringing this habitual interpretation mechanism into the wide-open space of our higher brain. As soon as I calm down, which can occur through the process of asking these questions, my neocortex comes back online and starts vetoing or calibrating the ego's concerns. Yes, I might be embarrassed. But that's probably the extent of the actual threat. As we'll see in the next step, I can't assume that my coworker "is out to get me." I am not likely to lose my job over that error or even suffer a significant performance rating drop. And even if I do take a hit on my appraisal, I can survive it. I can make this situation worse by going "high drama" with it and stuttering my way through the rest of the presentation. So I need to calm down and bring my neocortex and my Higher Self into the process of choosing how to behave. With the ego feeling heard and its fears visible, the Higher Self can create a wiser view. My Higher Self, and yours, is calmer and knows all of this instinctively. In fact, it even questions whether I looked bad in the first place!

Once you have identified the root cause of the ego's fears, you can work your way up from the deepest fear to the most shallow one with this more balanced point of view. Am I likely to die over this? No. Am I likely to lose my house over this? No. Am I likely to lose my job over this? No. Am I likely to suffer a significant decrease in my performance appraisal over this? No. Am I embarrassed—yes—but even that is optional. How I react to this is in my control. It all depends on how I interpret the situation. I have now taken the high ground—the view of Higher Self. In this step I find that at least 50% of the upset dissolves, and sometimes all of it.

Now that we've embraced the ego's concerns (Step 5) and looked deeply into the fears that go all the way down to death or abandonment (Step 6), we can now shift to Step 7: seeing the situation with new eyes.

Step 7. RE-FRAME (See with new eyes: the eyes of compassion and wisdom)

The art of reframing means to simply ask yourself: What else might be going on here that I don't know? How could I see this differently?

I paint watercolor landscapes as a hobby. I usually work from photographs of beautiful sunsets, flowers, mountains, and rivers. Initially, I'd try to duplicate what was in the photograph. This was fine for learning technique, but made for only average paintings. As I worked with various teachers, I realized that playing with perspectives made for much more interesting paintings. I started taking an interesting part of the painting and changing the relative proportions to help the viewer's eye focus on the area I had chosen as most important—the most valuable part for that moment. I can "tell a story" with my brush. We can do the same for the "paintings" we paint in our minds. When we interpret a situation, we are telling a story about it—we create an internal movie. There are the major and minor characters. We assign them motivations. We develop a primary and secondary storyline. There is a trajectory to the story. Often it is a good (me) versus evil (them) story with various sub-stories of allies and enemies. We create these stories and we believe them. In fact, we *forget* that we created them! We believe that what we created is just the way things are, and we believe the upset that results from these stories is an inevitable and logical outcome. "Anyone who lived in my shoes would feel this way." This is the voice of ego speaking, not the voice of Higher Self. Higher Self knows that we can "see with new eyes."

As we work with re-framing we learn to:

- See that we create the story, the interpretation of this event.
- Recognize that we are suffering upset from the story we have created.
- Understand that we can dis-create it; i.e., we can decide we don't like it and don't want it anymore. We can remove what is false. I sometimes say to my ego, "Sorry, but that is not the whole story here—there is more going on. Let that story go."
- Choose a new story, a new focal point for our mind that is empowering.

- Allow this new story to shift our hearts in transformative ways—letting forgiveness occur so fast it can feel surprising, almost without effort.

The usual tendency of ego is to blame others and absolve itself of any wrongdoing. Challenge the ladder of conclusions that your ego is busy climbing, and take a moment to consider other possibilities. To continue our example, the ego would automatically interpret a coworker pointing out a mistake in front of your boss as an attack. Here are some "alternate stories"—some reframes that demonstrate the beginnings of empathy/compassion for the coworker's point of view.

- Perhaps he is simply one of those people who cares about the little things, who sees mistakes and feels compelled to fix them. No harm intended—just a bit of perfectionism in his nature.
- Perhaps he feels the error might influence certain decisions and have a negative impact on the company.
- Perhaps the error relates to his area of responsibility, and he feels it makes him look bad.

Any of these could be a legitimate reason for his action, and holding these multiple interpretations in mind puts you in a position of greater wisdom. You realize that maybe, just maybe, there is more to this story than you first thought.

We can go further and reframe the story to see it even more powerfully by answering this question: What would it take for ME to do the exact same thing to someone else? Now, the ego usually rebels against this question and says, "I would never do that!" Here is where we have to breathe deeply, calm down, and ask our Higher Self to help us see this differently. I like to remind myself that if *any* of us would do something, *all* of us *could* do it under the right circumstance. Don't get distracted by wondering what this means about really awful people like genocidal dictators—we will address that later. For now, let's take on the more reasonable muscle-building exercise: the coworker again. And let's ask the questions at two levels of difficulty. At what we could call "Beginner level," we ask: why might I do the same thing to my coworker that he just did to me? And a beginner response tends to make me "right" for pointing out the mistake. Here are some samples:

- "Well, if I let that mistake slide it might cost the company a lot of money."
- "If the mistake was not pointed out now, Joe would get in trouble later—I was really protecting him."
- "That mistake on the slide made it look like my people didn't meet their target—when in fact they did. I was protecting my people."

You get the idea. Each of these beginner level responses lets me off the hook for meddling. They even glorify my meddling. What does the advanced level look like?

At the advanced level, we take the question deeper. We assume our intentions are *not* noble. What would cause us to do this? Can we own our own shadowy and less than wholesome motivations? Here are some examples of owning the whole truth—that yes, sometimes I do behave from not-very-kind motivations.

- I might correct someone else in front of the boss because I am jealous.
- I might lash out at my coworker because I've had a crummy day, a dozen things have gone wrong, I've been yelled at by a half-dozen people, and I took it out on him because I was mad and frustrated and I needed to vent.

The process I've been describing is obviously a long one that you may not have time to do in that very moment, in the midst of the meeting, while people are waiting for you to respond. But the act of even considering that there could be another interpretation is already a huge step. And as you learn to value this step, you'll find that you naturally want to continue the contemplation through to the advanced level. Because reframing is such a vital skill, I dig in a lot deeper regarding how to practice this in the coming chapters.

8. REFOCUS on something to be grateful for

What do we want to focus on? The ego always focuses on what is wrong. It tends to feel sorry for itself ("Poor me, look how I am treated!") or to blame others ("That's what wrong with this team; everyone is out for themselves.") Our Higher Self suspends judgment—not assigning blame, assuming evil intentions, or going into drama. It evaluates what is going on far more objectively and neutrally. And most importantly, the Higher Self can see what is good in a situation. It can see what is "right with the world."

Returning to watercolor painting, there is a useful analogy. A teacher told me about a fantastic way of turning a so-so painting into a great one—look for what is RIGHT in the painting. To do this it helps to hold a smaller matt up to the painting. For example, if a painting is done on paper that is twenty-two by thirty inches in size, you would normally matt it before framing it and include all of the paper minus about a quarter inch on each side. But if you matt the painting that way, it might be boring—or even bad. Maybe no one would want to buy it or hang it in his room. So try this exercise: Take an eight by ten inch matt or another significantly smaller size and look at the painting in segments. What is *right* with it? Usually some segment of the painting jumps out. "Wow! That is great. If I just touch this up a bit, it'll be a fantastic smaller painting." You find the best part of the painting and you cut away the rest! You focus on what is good. It is the same with the stories we tell ourselves.

When the ego is the director it tends to look for the high-drama, high-conflict parts of the story—what is bad, who is mean, and who is to blame. But when Higher Self is in charge it looks to find what is right, what is good in all the people and all the parts of this set of circumstances. It looks for something to be grateful for.

This is not always easy. And it requires some wisdom and balance. This step is not about ignoring relevant data. If someone is in fact (not just in speculation) trying to harm you, there is no point in denying that truth. But most of the time people are just being people, and we are creating our own suffering by telling overly dramatic stories about it. So what could I have focused on in our example with the coworker? I can think of a few things immediately:

- I am grateful that I have the poise to take the feedback gracefully, correct the error on the slide in question, and keep on going.
- I am grateful that people are awake enough to be listening, reading, and to notice an error (as opposed to sleeping through my presentation!)

- I am grateful that my boss is an understanding person who focuses on what matters
- I am grateful that my coworker has perfectionist tendencies. They are important in his job, and the company is better off for it.
- AND . . . I am always grateful for the chance to practice my spiritual weightlifting skills!

Again, we will explore this skill in more detail in the next chapter. For now, just know that refocusing on something to be grateful for is a beautiful partner to the Reframing step. In Step 7 we see other ways of interpreting the situation. In Step 8, we see something to be grateful for.

9. CHOOSE a spiritually intelligent response

Finally, the most important step is to choose a spiritually intelligent response—a response that does not come from your ego's survival-based reactions but from the wisdom of your Higher Self. The response could be as minimal as saying "thank you" and moving on, unruffled. Minimal, yes, but it makes all the difference in the world.

Learning to take these steps can produce dramatic results. And you don't need any special training or knowledge to practice these steps. You can start right away: when you put down this book, get off the bus or the subway, and go home to your family. Practice these steps in the emotionally charged situations you find yourself in every day—when your mother-in-law is visiting, when your boss is unreasonable, when your teenage daughter defies you. You can get there, one step at a time. And trust me, the impact it has will amaze you—the impact on your confidence, and on those around you. Being able to shift your trajectory in a heated moment, when your ego-train is gathering steam and pulling out of the station, is the essence of Spiritual Intelligence and can be a major turning point in your life.

TEN

Everyday SQ

"We want to be poets of our life — first of all in the smallest most everyday matters."

—Friedrich Nietzsche, *The Gay Science* (1882)

Developing Spiritual Intelligence, in all its many facets and expressions, is a lifetime's growth project. But as I have been explaining, it's also something you can put into practice every day and see immediate results in situations that are challenging, frustrating, or caught up in old habit patterns.

The nine-step process I describe in the previous chapter is what I came up with to put SQ into everyday practice in my own life and then to offer people who came to me for help. However, while I believe all the nine steps are important and should be practiced wherever possible to support your long-term development, I also appreciate that they may be too much for most people to remember or implement in heated moments or unexpected crises. Therefore, I came up with a shortcut that is more practical for daily use. This 4-step version is easy to remember, since its acronym spells S-O-U-L. What could be more appropriate, since the goal of this process is to act from the best part of your self?

The shortcut takes the most urgent parts of the 9-step process and condenses them for easy recall:

S = **S**top—interrupt the old habit pattern. Breathe. Ask Higher Self for help or Pray.

O = Observe what is going on—step back—call on your Witnessing/Observing Mind.

U = Understand that there is more here than the habitual understanding. See through their eyes.

L = Find a Loving (compassionate/wise) response, even if it is "I'll get back to you."

I teach these steps in many of my corporate trainings. In one class I worked with a group of nurses, and to help them remember I gave them each a little card on which the 9 steps were listed on one side and the S-O-U-L shortcut on the other. A week or so later, one of the participants told me a story: After the workshop she went back to her unit, and a coworker with whom she'd consistently clashed got right in her face. "My normal response would have been to yell right back," she said. "But I had your card in my hand, and I stopped. Then I just told myself to breathe, and I was able to observe what was happening. I stood there clutching your card and I didn't yell. I slowed down and listened. I was so proud of myself." That's how quickly you can start putting these steps into practice "in the heat of the moment." It doesn't take more than a few seconds to stop, take a deep breath, and choose a better response. I followed these two coworkers over the months that followed. Both received the training and they built a totally new relationship—one that was productive and friendly. It made life easier for them and their teams.

In this chapter I'd like to share some stories of how this process can be applied easily and effectively in everyday situations. Going through a debrief of an SQ21 assessment, attending a workshop on SQ, or talking with a certified SQ21 coach about issues or concerns can yield short-term and long-term benefits. Sometimes I am privileged to hear about the difference an exercise or insight made for someone. I will share a few of these so you can see how small changes can yield big rewards in your life. I hope that these stories will inspire and encourage you to begin to act with greater spiritual intelligence immediately.

Shifting from Ego to Higher Self Using Reframing

In coaching we talk about the importance of challenging our habitual interpretations of events and seeing differently. We will dig into how to practice this skill of reframing in Chapter 11, but for now I will illustrate its power with a story. In my workshops I often share with my clients a very moving tale from Stephen Covey's *The Seven Habits of Highly Effective People,* in which Covey describes how he was startled into a new and more loving perception of a situation involving some loud and irritating children.

I had told this story in one particular workshop with a group of nurses. A few weeks later, one of the nurses told me that after class she left the hospital and boarded the light rail city train for home. On the train was a couple with a young child. The child was screaming and screaming. She said her usual reaction would have been to judge the parents for not taking control. Then she remembered the Stephen Covey story. Covey had passed similar judgment on a man who let his children run wild on the subway—until he found out that those children had just lost their mother. This new information completely changed his perception. Recalling this story while faced with such a similar situation, the nurse stopped her usual ego thought and activated her observer self. This is the S and O of the S-O-U-L process. She looked more closely and saw that there were bandages under the child's shirt. She saw the distress on the parents' faces and leaned forward and said, "I am a nurse. Can I help you?" They explained that the child had just had outpatient surgery. They were on their way home and had to stop at a pharmacy to pick up the pain medication but it was clear that the medication from the hospital had worn off. The nurse said she immediately understood the situation differently (the U in the S-O-U-L). Her heart melted and her previous anger was gone. She gave the family whatever help and encouragement she could, and went home with an open heart instead of a contracted, annoyed ego. And she had helped that family. She was thrilled with the simple technique of Stopping, Observing, and Understanding before she acted. From those three steps she was able to take the fourth: to act with Love.

When I am asked "What is the difference between EQ and SQ?" I typically reply that EQ helps you manage your upsets appropriately. But when you do the work of SQ, the change goes deeper. You shed many of the anger triggers, which now seem trivial or silly. You remove unnecessary upset from your life, and that makes life a lot better.

Questions to ponder: Think of a person who irritates you. What "story" does your ego tell about his/her motivations or character? What assumptions are you making? Might your ego's version of reality be partially or totally incorrect? If you could see this with "new eyes" through your Higher Self, how might you feel?

Growing Your SQ and Sustaining Your Faith in Hard Times: Your Spiritual Support System

Another exercise I often use in my workshops focuses on spiritual support systems. It is designed to help people with several skills: hearing and acting from their Higher Self (skills 4 and 13), committing to their spiritual growth (skill 12), and sustaining faith during hard times (skill 15). We ask participants to take a blank sheet of paper and draw a circle and put their name in the circle. Around that circle we ask them to draw symbols representing all their sources of spiritual support. These can be activities (e.g., gardening, reading, singing, or religious or spiritual activities), people (e.g., friends, relatives, teachers), places they go (e.g., the ocean, sacred spaces), and other things like pets. They are then asked certain questions, such as how many sources of spiritual support they have, and are they well balanced. Conversation is helpful and most people add more ideas to their list as they listen to each other. They learn different ways that one can find spiritual support—from jogging (to clear out the voices of ego and its upsets) to meditation to being out in nature. And that nourishment can be found through previously unacknowledged channels.

One day I noticed a woman who became quite extroverted after this exercise—cracking jokes and being conversational in a way that felt a bit awkward in the group. At the end of the day she asked if she could make an appointment to talk with me. We met about a week later. She sat down and told me how much the workshop meant to her, and she immediately began crying. She said she was cracking jokes that day to keep from crying. This was because she'd had a shattering realization. She'd realized on that day that the only thing she had in her life was work. She was neglecting family, friends, and all other sources of personal spiritual support. She understood that this was why she was feeling so exhausted and was approaching burn-out. She wanted to change. We talked about things she could do differently. Months later, I saw her again and she was smiling and happy. She couldn't wait to tell me how she had made significant re-allocations of her time and energy and how wonderful it was. Life was so much richer for her now. I knew from those who worked around her that there was a positive change in her working relationships as well. And she reported that she and her daughter were now closer. She had looked at her spiritual support system and realized she didn't have one. She created one. And then she blossomed.

Questions to ponder: What is your spiritual support system? Do you have enough different avenues to find support, nourishment, renewal? Do you have organizations or people who help you to grow your SQ?

Compassionate Wise Behavior: Setting Healthy Boundaries

As I discuss more in the next chapter, my guiding question in life is "What would love do?" This makes sense, since behaving with high SQ is behaving with love (wisdom and compassion). Knowing the loving thing to do is not always easy. To develop SQ and put it into practice in everyday situations, we have to be willing to look deeply at our own motivations and assumptions.

As a subset of my guiding question, I have learned to ask myself, "Who am I REALLY helping here?" I learned this question in my early years of therapy. I realized that in relationships we often are engaged in a form of ego-based self-delusion. Here is an example: Your seven-year-old son Tommy comes home from school and tells you his school project is due tomorrow and he forgot all about it. He is upset, maybe even crying. You rush to help. The two of you go to the store, buy the poster board and colored paper, glue, and other supplies and do the work together. Ta dah! A poster explaining how cheese is made from milk has been assembled. A little part of you wonders, "Was that the right thing to do?" Ah well, you lost a little sleep, but at least little Tommy is happy and the teacher is happy and you feel like an involved and caring parent. But who were you really helping? Tommy or yourself?

Now imagine this is a 17-year-old son. Do you rush to help? Or do you let him suffer the consequences of bad planning, even if it affects his grade, which in turn affects his ability to get into his first choice college? What do you do when he is a freshman in college and the same thing happens? You can see the pattern.

I admit that I have a tendency to rescue. I rescue animals I see running lose in the neighborhood. I adopt dogs that need a home. And I often feel the urge to rescue people I barely know. Rescuing, I have learned, is not always the same as helping someone. I first deeply understood the harm that comes from rescuing young adults when I was coauthoring my first book, *Grown-Up Children Who Won't Grow Up*[41] with my friend, Dr. Larry Stockman. Larry taught me that parents who repeatedly rescue kids from their bad choices create incompetent adults. These "adult children" can behave in ways that are ridiculously entitled, or they may be severely depressed, or they may be highly manipulative (or all of the above). Clearly it was not the intention of the parents to create these characteristics in their children. The problem is that their good intentions were executed inside a faulty assumption: "good parents don't let their kids fail." And we all want our friends and neighbors to see us as good parents, don't we? This is why seeing our own worldview clearly (Skill 1) is so important. We also need to hear the voice of our ego as distinct from the voice of Higher Self (Skill 5).

Larry asked me one day as I was feeling the urge to rescue someone, "Who are you helping?" He helped me see that *I* was the one experiencing discomfort. I wanted to feel better. Rescuing the person would take away MY discomfort. I was helping me. The other person might be grateful *at that moment*. But I might actually be doing the other person harm. The person I rescued might be reinforced in believing: "I can't do it by myself. I am a failure." Is that loving? Who am I helping? I had to be willing to be with my own discomfort and say "no" if I wanted to be loving to this other person. And ultimately that was more loving to myself as well. As long as I was engaging in a bad pattern of rescuing I was reacting to fears of my ego. And I was keeping this person dependent on me while also resenting him for needing to be rescued. As the ego strives to relieve my discomfort it can create more discomfort for me down the road, and for those I am "helping." I still have to watch out for this voice of my ego self—the one that wants to relieve my short-term discomfort in seeing someone struggle by suggesting I should rescue him or her.

Many of us experience this. I see this a lot with bosses. An employee is missing a deadline and the boss steps in and rescues. What has the employee learned? If there was a real crisis, like a death in the family, the employee might have learned something good, like "the boss is really here for me when things are bad." But if it's the employee's laziness or a pattern of procrastination that is the cause, the employee is learning that using excuses and victim stories to get the boss to play "hero" is a good strategy. The boss may feel heroic and powerful in the moment. But over time, it's exhausting and keeps the boss from focusing on his or her valuable work. This behavior of rescuing is not serving the company, or the boss, or the employee. So how do good people get in these traps?

From family systems therapy comes a nice model that explains the ego trap we get caught in. It says that in any dysfunctional interaction (I would say an immature ego-based interaction) we have someone or some thing playing the role of "persecutor," someone is playing the "hero" or "rescuer," and someone is playing the role of "victim." We all tend to have a preferred role. Some people like playing the victim. Why? They get sympathy, help from others, and are not held accountable. Some people like being the hero. Why? They get praise, and feel powerful and useful. Most of us would not see ourselves as the persecutor. But I can own that role. There are times when I have spoken unkindly about another person, and if they were in the room, or if they heard about what I said, they would feel persecuted by me.[42] I receive ego-gratification even from the persecutor role because I feel "superior" to the person I am judging and saying harsh things about.

I have learned the power of this question in my own life. In coaching and consulting, inside an SQ context where we have established that the goal is to behave with love (wisdom and compassion), I ask my clients this same question: Who are you helping here? Eyes often fly wide open when they realize they are helping relieve *their own discomfort* first and foremost. Then the questions become, "How do I break this pattern?" and "How can I say no to this person?" Here is the importance of setting boundaries with love, not anger. We might role-play the WRONG way to do this (this is always a bit fun and freeing, and relieves the tension). I suggest people let the ego run wild for a moment. Let's say that you are caught in the rescuer trap. What would be a deliciously ego-based angry and mean way to tell "John" that you will not be rescuing him this time? We might come up with this kind of ridiculous imaginary scene.

- I would surprise him with the news that I wouldn't be rescuing him again.
- I wouldn't tell him why I was changing or provide any context for why it was important for him and his success at the company that he learn to stand on his own two feet.
- I'd tell him in public.
- I'd wait until I knew it was too late for him to possibly get the job done.
- I'd ridicule him, or belittle him for previous failures.
- I'd use body language that made it clear that I was disgusted with him.

Sometimes letting the ego "out of the closet" for a while can help us see how NOT to do something. Then we can say, okay, what would your Higher Self do? What is the loving thing to do in this situation? And it's pretty obvious that what the boss should do is the reverse of all of the above.

Questions to ponder: Whom do you like to rescue? Who or what do you like to blame when you are feeling victimized? Who do you like to yell at when you are mad? In each of these cases, can you see that this is the voice of the ego suggesting a line of defense for you that is not loving to you or the other person?

Using SQ to Motivate Deep Change

I once had a Senior Vice President of Human Resources ask me, "What is different in what you do versus what other coaches and consultants do? Why is SQ different or better than regular team-building or leadership development?" My answer was: we get at deeper meaning-making structures. We tap the noblest aspirations of people. And from there, THEY are motivated to change. More classical or traditional interventions may try to motivate people by using pep talks and incentive programs, corporate goals and aspirations for promotions. SQ holds out the possibility that people can live their own lives in the direction of becoming more like their own heroes and spiritual exemplars. This provides a far more powerful personal motive for change than more typical interventions." How did the SVP of HR reply? He said, "I agree with you."

The everyday practice of SQ depends on awakening and cultivating this deeper motive within yourself. I will illustrate how I tap this desire to "be our highest selves" by presenting two examples through two different types of people. I will call them Jarod and Sonya. (To protect the privacy of my clients, each of these characters is a composite and is not intended to represent any actual individual). The problems they encounter are ones I see frequently. They each represent a "stance" or perspective on life that is currently blocking their SQ development. These two characters represent two contrasting "spiritual approaches" that I often see in good people trying to do good work. These are cases where ego has hijacked spiritual-sounding language, and people end up being ineffective and unhappy, driven by a defensive ego self. Yet in each case, with a small shift in perspective, they can see a healthier path forward.

Jarod: The Noble Hero—Defender of the Powerless

Jarod is a male name, but this character could just as easily be a woman. Jarod has a fear of being stepped on or mistreated that goes back to his early childhood. He believes in sticking up for the underdog and standing up to authority whenever his integrity is challenged. His ego defense mechanism is completely understandable. It is also below his conscious level of awareness. In other words, it runs him, driving his behavior habits. His ego is always on guard like a street fighter with fists always raised, watching for instances where people are "doubting his word" or pushing him around. When you are around him you get the feeling that you don't want to mess with him. He is quick to interrupt. He is also quick with a joke and in many other ways a very likeable guy.

Jarod extends this vigilance to some other people—even if they don't ask for his help. He is quick to defend anyone he sees as less powerful against those in power. On the plus side, this has led him to do some impassioned volunteer work through his neighborhood food pantry. He works hard to raise money and get food donations to keep the local food pantry well stocked. Sometimes he fills in as a driver for a food route that brings prepared meals to the elderly. He has shown up at city council meetings to express his opinion about budget cuts for these programs. He has received awards from the nonprofits he volunteers with. These are proudly displayed in his office.

On the negative side, he has recently received performance feedback from his supervisor about his quick temper and his tendency to alienate coworkers. He is perceived as self-righteous and a bully. His boss has asked him to listen better and compromise more, and has told him he needs to work with a coach because the problem has become too serious to leave him on his own to sort it out. The boss acknowledges that Jarod is a hard worker who produces a high volume. But the price of his aggressive style is getting too high for the company to tolerate.

Jarod discounts this supervisor feedback: "What do you expect?" He is almost proud of the negative feedback he is getting since he feels that "those in power" shouldn't like him. If they did like him, it would mean he was "selling out to the system," and the system, as far as he can see it, smells bad. His story about business and how it works is that the rich take care of the rich, and the powerful take care of the powerful. Thus he is trapped in seeing his best asset—his desire to do right by the powerless—as inherently resulting in lower performance ratings from management.

Jarod knows he needs his paycheck. And he doesn't hate his company. But he also doesn't want to sacrifice his values. He believes he is living a noble life—in SQ language, he believes he is living from his highest self. But is he?

I would suggest that Jarod's ego self is still running the show. Ego is hiding behind noble-sounding stories to work a fear-based agenda. Jarod is caught in the ego-gratification of "being a hero." A therapist might say that Jarod rescues others in order to heal a past where no one rescued him.

There is a problem with this, of course. Heroes only have people to rescue if there are victims. This means the ego-self has to encourage other people to be "needy victims" for him to have his role. And victims in this process need to have a persecutor—someone or something they can blame for their problems. The hero then jumps in and saves the victims from the persecutor (the system, the boss, a coworker, the overly demanding customer, and so forth). This keeps the drama going.

As a coach, I first appreciate what is wonderful about each client. Jarod is passionately committed to being a good human being. I would tell Jarod how I admire his desire to protect and serve others. I would ask him what motivates this in him. And he would probably tell me beautiful stories about valuing justice for all, equality, and fairness. I would encourage him to make a list of all these values. I would repeat these back to him. I would ask him if he felt that this was a way that he demonstrated his love for other humans. He might be startled by the "L" word, but would probably say "yes."[43] This would begin an ongoing conversation about what love is, and what it is not.

As I mentioned earlier, a commonly held spiritual principle is the Golden Rule—typically stated as "do unto others as you would have them do unto you." I would ask Jarod if he agreed with this and he would say "Yes, I do." I would ask him, "How do you select a birthday gift for someone you love?" Jarod would say he would select something the person would like to receive. I might ask if he has ever heard the story about a husband who loves to fish buying his non-fishing wife a bass boat for her birthday. We would chuckle about the self-focused mind that might think a bass boat was a good idea! We could imagine the husband who gave this gift saying, "Well honey, you always say you want to spend more time with me. This way we can spend more time together!" I would ask Jarod to tell me what might be wrong about this gift selection. Jarod would rightly point out that the husband picked out something *he* wanted. He didn't consider what *she* wanted.

Jarod and I would discuss how there are a million ways we can give our loved ones, coworkers, and friends "bass boats." We deliver to them what we think we'd want in the same situation. In his role as hero/protector, Jarod is confusing the other person with the wounded child inside him whom his ego is still trying to protect. Depending on the depth of the wounded child issues, I might suggest that Jarod take these issues into therapy to address them. Having "seen with new eyes," Jarod would now be open to seeing his own rescuing behaviors as "bass boat" behaviors.

Here is the ideal application of the Golden Rule. It is sometimes improved upon and called the Platinum Rule: Do unto others as they would be done to. In other words, don't buy your wife a bass boat if she hates to fish. Give her what she would love having. This requires that we put ourselves in the other person's shoes (Skill 7: Understanding the Worldview of Others). I would say "do no harm" is a basic boundary. If your habit of taking care of your wounded inner child by protecting others is encouraging codependent victim-type behaviors in them, no one is winning. You are not, they are not, and the company is not.

With these insights, Jarod can begin a journey that will give him room to grow his SQ for a lifetime. Hopefully, Jarod can have compassion for the part of himself that wants to be the hero and protect people. And he now can tease apart *intention* from *skillful means*. Intending to help is noble, but with unskillful implementation he is getting undesirable results and creating a win/lose situation with his boss. We'd want to practice his new worldview and skills by looking at multiple examples where there was an opportunity to act like "old Jarod" and talk about how "new Jarod" or Higher Self Jarod would want to respond. In so doing, we are taking his existing noble intentions—the desire to help and protect—and placing it under the guidance of his Higher Self rather than his fearful ego (Skills 5 and 13). From this vantage point he can see how to truly show up as a compassionate, wise, and peaceful person who makes sustainable differences in the world (Skill 19). And in the process he can learn the skills to listen and work well with others in pursuit of a common goal (Skill 18). He will be perceived as less of a bully, and more as a partner on a team. He can improve his performance rating *and* be the beautiful human being he always wanted to be.

Sonya: The Peace-Maker

Sonya is a gentle soul who loves to get along with people. (As with Jarod, Sonya represents many clients and could be a man or a woman.) She greatly values harmony and avoids conflict whenever possible. Her fear is that people won't like her. She learned as a child that things work best if everyone likes her. Her ways of getting people to like her include going out of her way to please people (like bringing donuts every Friday), doing too much to help others with their work, or bending where she shouldn't bend. This is her dominant ego defense. Her ego feels it is protecting her. But in the long run it has made Sonya resentful. She feels that no one appreciates her, or reciprocates her help, or makes an effort to do things *her* way. She always has to take care of others. She is feeling tired, sad, and victimized. Yet she rationalizes that her path is a "higher path" of service.

In this case, Sonya might self-refer for life coaching. She is exhausted and discouraged and wants to know what she is doing wrong. As with Jarod, the goal first is to appreciate her strengths and noble intentions. Clarifying her values improves her self-esteem as we begin the journey of discussing who she wants to be and how she wants to show up. She wants to be loving—that is immediately clear. And she wants to do "the right thing"—not the easy thing. She is turned off by people who are lazy or selfish. Those are real hot buttons for her.

We talk about to whom she acts loving. How does she express her care and concern? Does she show any love to herself? How does she do that? In this process, the theme of sacrificing self to stay safe (be liked) eventually emerges. We can then talk about the juicy topic of setting boundaries with love. We surface her own limiting beliefs (Skill 1) and look at how they conflict with her life purpose (Skill 2) and values (Skill 3). She took the SQ21 and scored poorly on complexity of thinking. She was initially upset by this. As we discuss the questions and her answers, it becomes clear that her disposition is to "follow the rules no matter what." I ask her to name her spiritual heroes. Her heroes are Martin Luther King Jr., Gandhi, and Nelson Mandela.

When I ask her what she admires about them, she replies that they all made the world a better place, through nonviolence. Then I ask her if her heroes ever broke any rules, and I see the "light bulb" moment occur. She recognizes that they did, but only under guidance of some very high principles driven by love and Higher Self. Social justice and civil disobedience were advocated in a nonviolent way. Through looking more closely at the examples of those people she most admires, she sees that blind acquiescence to requests from others is how she "follows the rules"—and that there might be other options.

Using her own desire to be more like Gandhi, for example, we talk about how to set very strong boundaries in nonviolent ways. Gandhi was an inspiration to Martin Luther King Jr. and to Nelson Mandela. Her Higher Self selected those heroes because they are pointing the way. They could be instructional guides for her on how to set boundaries with love. She agrees that she needs to learn to listen to the voice of her Higher Self (Skill 5), act from it (Skill 13), and love people in a healthy way (Skill 19). She uses the guiding question "What would Gandhi do?" and over time develops more complexity of thinking (Skill 4). She changes her assumptions about how the world works (Skill 1) and becomes a calmer and more centered person (Skill 20). The changes are gradual but steady from that day forward.

In his much-loved bestseller *The Road Less Traveled,* M. Scott Peck wrote that love "is the will to extend one's self for the purpose of nurturing one's own or another's spiritual growth."[44] His definition really hit home for me. He says that love is not a "feeling"—as in "falling in love;" nor is it neediness. Sometimes we confuse "I need you" with "I love you." Lust or need is not love. Love, he points out, is a choice we make, an act of will. It means doing the right thing for someone even if you don't like the person. Doing the right thing even if it is not the easy thing to do. And love nurtures one's own and the other's spiritual growth. So love is not self-damaging. It is a win-win deal when seen from the right perspective. Sometimes it may feel like a sacrifice. But that is probably the voice of the ego speaking. In the end, when we act from this kind of love, everyone wins. Love nourishes me and it nourishes you. So we hold this in mind as we look at how to apply spiritual intelligence in our lives—where is the win-win? If there are three people involved, where is the win-win-win? "Winning" in this context doesn't mean making everyone happy. It means doing what is right—loving—for each person. Sometimes the most loving thing we can do is to say "no" to someone. Sonya exemplifies the need to learn how to say "no."

I meet many people like Sonya and have seen many such deeply touching "light bulb moments" with clients who connect their spiritual heroes with the solution to their dilemma. They have found the deep inner motivation to make the change that most serves them. And it serves those they love and work with as well.

Now that you have heard these stories of the benefits of SQ, in Chapter 11 we turn to the most popular and powerful exercises I teach people for overall "spiritual weightlifting." You can begin to build your own SQ today. Why wait?

ELEVEN

Three Core Exercises to Support SQ Development

"The real voyage of discovery consists not in seeking new landscapes, but in having new eyes."

—Marcel Proust, *La Prisonnière*

Spiritual weightlifting, like its physical counterpart, is a complex process involving many different muscles. Just as you wouldn't go to the gym and only work on one bicep, day after day, you cannot expect any one practice or exercise to be enough to develop your SQ. There are many exercises and practices you can engage with to build your spiritual strength and cultivate your skills.[45] But there are some exercises that are foundational—that develop the spiritual equivalent of a strong core. In this chapter I share three exercises that I have found most helpful in my own development and in my work with clients:

1. Asking a Guiding Question
2. Reframing
3. Developing an Attitude of Gratitude

These exercises are designed to support your overall SQ, but especially the ability to listen to and act from your Higher Self, to see your own and another's worldviews, to live according to your values, and to behave with wisdom and compassion while maintaining calm centered presence (Skills 1, 3, 5, 7, 13, 19, 20).

It takes disciplined practice to make SQ real. In Chapter 9 we looked at the 9 steps to shift from ego to Higher Self. I teach full-day workshops on these 9 steps where I share exercises that help with each step. Obviously we can't go into the same depth in one chapter, but the high-impact exercises that follow are ones that you can do on your own.

EXERCISE 1: Asking a Guiding Question

Setting an intention for my life and for each day in my life is a crucial piece of my own "inner GPS" process. If I don't know where my "true north" is, I cannot move in that direction. My "true north" is Love. My highest intention is that I want to express spiritual intelligence, which means I want to act with love (wisdom and compassion). When I am confused and upset I need something simple and easy to remember. So my "guiding question" in a tough moment is: "What would Love do?" This orients me to my intention—to show up as love in as many moments as possible. Then I go through the 9-step process (or the 4-step shortcut in high-pressured situations). I practice "Stop, Breathe, Pray," and I work to shift.

For some people the guiding question might be: "What would Jesus do?" or something more personal like, "What would Dad do?" Let's find a question that works for you.

Get out a blank piece of paper and work items A through D below.

A: Who are your heroes?

Write down the names that come up for you. As you think about this, consider what human beings, alive or dead, fictional or real, you have most admired. Admired is the key word. You might ask, "Who would I most like to be like?" or "Who are the spiritual exemplars I most look up?" If you have only one name that is okay. If you have two or more that is fine too.

B: List the character traits or behaviors that have caused you to admire this person or these people.

You don't have to line up the traits by person (if you have two or more people on your list). Just list the traits you admire about them in general.

C: Looking at those traits, circle up to three that are the "most important" traits.

If you see a theme emerging, for example, many of the traits point back to a core idea like compassion, you can summarize the theme.

D: **Write a first draft of your guiding question by completing this: "What would ____ do?"**

You can insert the name of one of your heroes or the theme or most important trait or value that emerged from this exercise.

This is a great beginning. To apply this in your life, keep going with E through G below.

E. If you have a business card with a blank back (or equivalent size piece of paper) write the question on the back of that card and carry it in your wallet or pocket or car for a week. Look at it periodically. Improve it as you feel moved to do so.

F. After you have lived with it for a week and feel you have a solid agreement with yourself that this is your "true north," begin asking the question whenever you feel upset. "What would ___ do?" See if this calls forth your Higher Self voice and helps you see that your ego self might be pushing you in a direction that is away from your true north. Don't get mad at your ego (it doesn't help the process). Just notice. And, if possible, choose to move in the direction your Higher Self seems to be speaking up for.

G. Refine this process over time with the support of practice and experience. Our initial steps are often to just do the *opposite* of whatever the ego says. This may or may not be the best thing to do in a situation. Notice those times when you are acting from a truly wise and compassionate place (high SQ) versus just reacting in the opposite direction of the ego voice. You can tell by how you feel and how skillfully you handle the situation. Do not get discouraged. When we try something new—like riding a bike—we typically make mistakes, fall over, and skin our hands and knees. It's part of the process. None of it is wasted if we learn from it. You might have done the right thing and just not yet done it skillfully; you might need practice. Or you might have made a choice that was still not a Higher Self choice because you were merely reacting against the ego self's idea. Tune in to

your inner wisdom and tease apart the situation logically to figure out what other options you may have missed. Use the
reframing practices described below to help you with this con-
tinual refinement process. I do not believe I will ever be done trying to figure out: "Was there a MORE loving option?"

The point here is not perfectionism, or getting stuck in analysis. I
hold my guiding question as an intention that I take seriously. I want to
continually improve. And I must show compassion towards myself—
towards my own imperfections—in this process.

EXERCISE 2: REFRAMING

Expanding the Heart and Mind with Reframing: What It Is and Why It Matters:

The term "reframing" comes from psychology. It is a metaphor for how
we "frame a situation" just as we frame a picture. When we take a painting to the frame shop, the technician helps us select a frame and matt.
We are looking for a matt and frame that will flatter the painting, present
it in the best possible way. This means the combination of frame and
matt should be compatible with the colors of the painting—especially the
colors we like looking at. So if I want the blues of the ocean to "pop"
because I value them, I might echo that color of blue in the matt I select.

We do the same thing with our minds. We focus on the stories and
interpretations that we like. And we "frame" stories to emphasize our
own interpretations.

Take this common example: Imagine Evelyn is going through a
divorce. Which do you think most likely happens when her best friend
asks her how she is doing?

A: She tells her friend how hard it is for her estranged husband to
be living alone. How he misses the daily craziness with their
kids. How he has felt estranged from her for a long time. He has
felt like a failure, and has been burying that feeling in dating
and drinking too much.

B. She tells her friend how lonely she is and what a jerk her husband is being about visitation. She tells her about how sad the
kids are and how angry that makes her at her husband. She

explains how her lawyer is trying to work with her husband's lawyer but that he is being impossible. Her friend takes her side and agrees that her husband and his lawyer are both being jerks.

C. Evelyn, while clearly sad, tells her friend the facts as separate things from the feelings she has about the facts and owns full responsibility for things she is interpreting that may or may not be true. She has a good long cry on the shoulder of her best friend who allows her to be fully present to her grieving process without inflaming things or adding her own upset to the mix. Evelyn returns to her kids more peaceful, less angry, and more able to be present to their grieving processes.

Most of us would do "B," and most of our good friends, in an effort to be supportive, would be tempted to "side with us" against our spouse. Divorces are usually painful experiences and we need friends to hear our pain. There is nothing inherently untrue about the perspective in B, as long as Evelyn sees it as an interpretation. Being without a spouse at home is a fact. Being "alone" is technically not a fact (her kids are home with her) but "being alone" *is* an expression of a feeling—feeling alone and lonely. These feelings are normal and should be processed openly rather than buried. The kids probably are sad, as most kids would be in this situation. It seems that she is blaming her husband for "making them sad"—which is an interpretation/defense of the ego to allocate blame to another. It would be more true to say the situation is hard, and they are sad about it, and maybe even angry at their parents. And these feelings too are understandable.

We can tell these are interpretations by asking, "Would the husband see it this way too?" or "Would any objective observer see that the kids' sadness as 'clearly' the husband's fault?" Because the answer to these questions is no, we therefore see that the position Evelyn is holding is clearly her interpretation.

The ego over-simplifies, over-dramatizes, and interprets things in order to keep us "safe" (i.e., without blame). The problem is that when we assign blame, not only are we potentially inaccurate, but we are also giving away our power. If it is "his fault" that the kids are sad, then the implied solution is for him to "come home, change who he is, be the kind of person I want him to be and the kind of dad I want him to be, and then the kids will be happy."

These are the kinds of interpretations I am making, you are making, we all are making. Why does that matter? Because once we OWN that we are making the interpretations, we can choose a new interpretation: we can reframe the situation through new eyes. And in that CHOICE lays tremendous power. See some examples of different interpretations in the table below.

Immature "Ego Stories"	Reframing to See with the Eyes of Higher Self
Knee-jerk or habit—the stories and interpretations come readily to mind	I hesitate to interpret anything too quickly (unless immediate action is needed). I assume "I do not know what this means." And I hold the uncertainty (open mind) while I contemplate the data and many possible interpretations
Focuses on what the OTHER person or people did wrong. Or on how unfair the world is. Does NOT focus on what I (or we) did to contribute to the problem.	Sees everyone involved as probably contributing to the situation—including, and maybe especially, looking to see how I (or we) might have created this situation
Sees only the bad things that will come from this. Inflames negative emotions: fear, anger, worry, sadness, hopelessness, revenge, jealousy, etc.	Seeks to see even-handedly—the harm and the gifts. What gifts might be embedded in this? Even if the situation is horrible, something good might eventually come from it. Seeks to find the positive emotions of hope, gratitude, empathy, compassion, etc.
Wants "justice" in the sense of revenge—even if that is achieved through bad-mouthing the person rather than actually doing something to them that is physical.	Seeks to find interior reframing and forgiveness of the situation first (a gift we give ourselves) before seeking reconciliation or other solutions.

Immature "Ego Stories"	Reframing to See with the Eyes of Higher Self
Anger motivates action. Limbic system dominates. Neocortex (higher brain functions) may be hijacked or engaged only in service of the anger. Low IQ or misdirected IQ. Low EQ and SQ. Thought processes NARROW.	Where I stand in my mind/heart matters. If time can possibly allow, I fix my interior before I act. Then I bring multiple intelligences to bear on the situation. IQ engaged along with EQ and SQ (wisdom and compassion, inner calm). Thought processes WIDEN.
Confirmation Bias in full swing: I seek only data that confirms my dislike of this person and my own interpretation of events. I refuse to see or acknowledge disconfirming data. I get upset when people try to challenge my habitual assumptions. ("You are with me or against me").	I actively seek data—especially that which might DIS-confirm my assumptions and habitual interpretations. I find relief in breaking old assumptions
I refuse to take responsibility for the problem or situation. It is clearly the other person's fault, or just "what happened."	I find RELIEF in finding elements where I created the problem or helped to co-create it. This is because owning my co-creation means I can choose again and choose more wisely. I can dis-create this situation, or at least not create it again with other people. And each time I learn something I am GRATEFUL for the wisdom and compassion it brings.

Immature "Ego Stories"	Reframing to See with the Eyes of Higher Self
Low PQ or physical intelligence: Body is flooded with harmful hormones due to chronic activation of sympathetic nervous system (fight-or-flight system). Immune system suppressed. Higher blood pressure, pulse, respiration. Respiration shallow. Muscles tight, jaw clenched. Digestive problems may result. Sleep disruptions may occur.	Higher PQ: Minimal time in fight-or-flight. Conscious reactivation of parasympathetic nervous system. Calms blood pressure, etc. Body is more centered and so is the mind. Health not compromised.

Assuming you are convinced of the value of reframing, how do you do it? The two techniques that work best for me are: Creating Alternate Stories and Putting Myself in the "Bad Guy" Role. I usually do these in this order, since creating alternate stories is easier, and supports my ability to put myself in the "bad guy" role.

Technique One: Creating Alternative Stories

Think of a scenario that will likely be upsetting to your ego. It may be work-related or it may be generic. Take a moment to come up with a specific scenario that has resonance for you. Maybe it's an incident with a colleague in the office; maybe it's a frustrating person holding up the line at the store; maybe it is a parent not controlling his children, as in the example from the previous chapter. To illustrate how the reframing practice works, here is a generic example:

> Imagine you are on your way home from work. You are tired. It's been a long day. You cannot wait to get home, eat a quick dinner, and relax in front of the TV with your family. You are on the highway. A thunderstorm occurs and the rain comes down so hard that even with your wipers on maximum speed you have trouble seeing through your windshield. You can't see the lane markers very well. You have slowed down and so have the cars around

you. You can see tail lights, but not much else. You consider pulling off the road onto the shoulder, but you are not able to see clearly where the shoulder is and are worried you might end up in the dirt or trees. You are trying to decide what to do when suddenly you see something in front of you that causes you to brake hard and veer to the right. You bounce around and the car comes to a sudden halt. You are off the road with the car angled downward in a drainage ditch. The nose of your car is in the water, but the back tires are still out of the ditch. You open the door of your car and step out. Your clean shoes sink ankle deep in the mud. The rain is pouring down your face. The thunder claps loudly and you startle. You turn to see what on earth blocked you on the highway. You see a four car pile-up on the highway.

Once you have established your scenario, deliberately take on the "voice of the upset ego" and come up with every negative story you can possibly think of. If it helps, imagine you are some obnoxious character you know from television or movies or books. When we first begin seeking to hear these voices it can be fun and helpful if you have a friend or partner to do it with. You can keep the whole process feeling safe by keeping it impersonal and treating it as if you were writing scripts for some self-centered or immature characters you know from fiction or real life (no names please!).

This exercise can actually be a lot of fun. When I do this in workshops, the room gets pretty noisy. After about ten minutes I ask people to share. Here are some typical "upset ego" stories people might share in response to the scenario I described:

- Why me? This kind of ___ always happens to me! Wasn't work awful enough today? Can't a guy/gal just go home and relax?
- Who are these jerks that just turned my day into ___?
- Who can I sue? Someone is going to pay for the damage to my car. And my shoes for that matter! And this suit is ruined. I am calling my lawyer.
- I am a lawyer—and this is great. I can give out my business cards. Someone will be suing someone over this!
- Stupid darn drivers . . . if they can't drive right they shouldn't be on the road. Look at all the trouble they've caused!

- Now what am I going to do? Who is going to pick up the kids from daycare? How do I get a tow truck in this storm? It'll be hours before I can get one.

- This storm couldn't have waited 25 more minutes? I would have been home by then.

- Super. Not only will this screw up the evening, but I don't have insurance because that idiot agent didn't get it set up in time. So I won't have a car. And now with this rain I'll catch a cold and miss work and get in trouble with my boss. Life stinks.

You get the idea. The point is to create whining, self-focused, manipulative, high-drama stories that explain what the event means. Some people create stories worthy of a daytime soap opera, with love triangles, kidnappings, amnesia, and on and on! When I ask people to volunteer to read their stories out loud, usually the class is mildly amused to outright laughing. Typically the stories get increasingly melodramatic as we go around the room. Often "facts" that were not in the story itself are fabricated to support a point of view. This is all great learning, because it allows us to see our egos with a little distance, and hopefully with some compassionate humor.

When you have come up with a good array of stories, the next step is to notice the pattern you see in the stories. You should be able to see how all these stories inflame your negative emotions and can become a vicious downward cycle. This can help you to acknowledge that you, like all of us, have the potential to "go all ego drama" on any interpretation.

The next step is to come up with Higher Self interpretations of the same incident. Try to think of more compassionate stories, and to see if there is anything for you to be grateful for in the situation. Here are some examples of how that might look for the scenario in our example:

- I am not injured. I am so grateful. The car took some damage but that can be repaired. Shoes can be replaced. I am grateful to be alive and ABLE to see my family later today.

- I am grateful that I had my seat belt on and that I am ok.

- I am grateful that it wasn't any worse than this. I am so lucky I wasn't one of the cars on the highway. It looks bad in that wreck.

- I am grateful that I have car insurance.
- I am grateful that I have family and friends who will be happy to see me. And I can't wait to see them. I need to tell them all how much I love them.
- I am reminded of how short life can be. I need to treasure it more. (Some people add: "Thank you God for the wake-up call")
- I am grateful I am here to help these people in the accident. What should I do to help? Should I put out flares to help other cars not rear-end these cars and not go off in the ditch like me? Is anyone injured? Has anyone called 911 yet?

And one of the most touching Higher Self voices I have heard:

- I am a nurse. I have emergency room experience. Thank God for my training. I am here and unharmed because Spirit wanted me to help these people. Someone here needs my help. Thank you God for putting me here today so I can be of service.

Once you have come up with a list of Higher Self interpretations, ask yourself, how do these make you feel? Try to name your emotions." I find that people will usually list a variety of positive emotions: relaxed, grateful, happy, peaceful, inspired, caring, compassionate, and so on. They also list a few negative emotions that are triggered by care and concern, for example, "I am worried for the health of the people in the accident."

Lastly, compare the first set of ego stories and the emotions they generated (negative, self-focused) to the emotions generated by the Higher Self stories (positive and/or other-focused). This should give you a powerful insight into the relationship between what we think about and what we feel. The power you have to create your own upset, or your own joy—to engage your compassion or turn it off—should become more apparent. In this way, the power of SQ to help us manage our EQ becomes clear.

Technique Two: Putting Yourself in the "Bad Guy" Role

In this more advanced technique, we bring the voice of the Higher Self more clearly and powerfully into focus. Once again, you can come up with your own scenario, but to illustrate the exercise, place yourself mentally in this scenario:

You have stopped on the way home from work to pick up some food at the grocery store. You are in a hurry to get home where everyone is waiting for you so dinner can be cooked. You have five or six items, and you get in the express lane to check out and pay for your groceries. The sign over the lane clearly says "Max 12 items." You notice there is a person already checking out in this lane who clearly has at least twenty items in their cart. You feel your irritation rising. To make things worse, once the clerk announces the amount due the person pulls out a checkbook and begins to fill out a check.

Take out a piece of paper and write down the ego's reactions. Allow its voice to be as whiney, or irritated, or judgmental as you can come up with. Let it be melodramatic. Imagine the various snide remarks this ego voice might want to make to the cashier and the customer. As with the last exercise, if you think, "Well, I'd never say that kind of stuff," then imagine the most obnoxious character you've ever seen on TV or in the movies and put the words in their mouth. One client told me that he would have (and in fact had in similar situations) pointed to the sign and told the customer to have some respect for other people. Another client said he might have followed the person out into the parking lot and told the person off all the way to his or her car. Anger can hijack us and make us act in ways that in the calm light of day are clearly over-reactions. Sometimes the stories people tell in workshops make others laugh, which is okay. We need to learn to see, and also to smile at, this aspect of our humanness. The most important part is, we have to SEE it. Awareness precedes our ability to change anything. This is Skill 5 in action: learning to hear the voice of the ego self.

Once you feel you have run out of ideas for the ego's voice, turn to the voice of your Higher Self. But this time, we'll try a more advanced technique.

Ask yourself this question: "What would it take for ME to do this obnoxious thing that this customer is doing?" In other words, what would be going on with me if I was actually the one with twenty-plus items in my basket in the express lane writing out a check?

Now, if you are like most people, your ego voice immediately protests. Especially since you've just been berating this imaginary customer as you took on the voice of the ego self. Your ego voice might say, "I am a thoughtful person! I would never do that." If you hear your ego voice say something like that, speak to it as if it were a frightened child. Tell it something like this: "I hear you. I know you are worried about looking like a bad person. But trust me, there is nothing to fear here. This is just an exercise. If we do it well, we could become an even better person—one who has compassion and wisdom. So don't worry. There is no risk here. All is well. I am in charge. You can relax and go to sleep for a little while." I have conversations like this with my ego self all the time. In the 9-step process, this is part of Step 5: Acknowledging the Fears of the Ego Self.

After your ego has settled down a bit, go back to the question. "Why would I be the person in the express lane with too many items, writing a check?" What would have to be going on in my life? What would the story be that would explain this?

I would ask that you work on this for a while BEFORE you turn the page to see the answers other people have offered to this question.

Here are some examples of reasons people have given in my workshops as to why they might be the one behaving in this way:

- I am in a huge hurry. I have a major family crisis going on. Someone is in the hospital. I have to get home and take care of the kids and then rush to the hospital. I don't have enough cash with me. My credit cards are maxed out. I have to write a check. I hope it doesn't bounce . . .

- I have had a really bad day. I have a migraine coming on. I know I only have about thirty minutes left before I can't even see to drive. I need to get home right away. All I have with me is my driver's license and my checkbook—so I have to write a check.

- I was in the other line but the cashier waved me over into his line. There was a long line in the regular lane, but he had no one in his—so he told me to come on over. Then this other person came up behind me and gave me a dirty look. I was too embarrassed to explain.

- I am from another country. I can speak enough English to get by—but I can't read it.

- I am very old. I can't see very well. I am so glad people are patient with me. I never trusted credit cards. I like to write a check so I know where my money is going.

- I am from this country, but I never learned to read. I am functionally illiterate. But I am too embarrassed to ask for help. So I try to figure out what is going on and follow the rules as best I can.

- I am really distracted with physical pain. I am so worried that my health problem is back. I am worried it might be fatal this time. I am on the verge of tears. I am so worried I didn't even see the sign and the cashier didn't say anything to me. I should have started writing the check out as soon as I got in line, but I can't think straight today. I was startled when the cashier asked me how I was going to pay. How can I deal with all of this? I am so distraught . . .

In workshops, as we go through everyone's stories about "what would it take for me to do this behavior" you can feel the emotional tone in the room shift. After getting ourselves worked up with emotional upset, suddenly there are "light bulb moments" going on all around the room.

"Wow . . . it could be me. I could do this." I usually ask if any of these scenarios have happened to anyone in the room? Usually the answer is yes. We all break the rules sometimes. Sometimes it's accidental. Sometimes it is intentional. What is true is that we don't actually know what is going on with that customer in front of us in line. What if one of the scenarios above was true? It is possible this person is a selfish jerk (the ego's story). But it is even more possible that one of these other stories, or another one we can't imagine, is the truth.

Remember the story I mentioned in the previous chapter about how Stephen Covey felt when the man on the train with the children shattered his assumptions? I prefer not to feel like an idiot. I prefer not to get myself all worked up over stories I am telling myself about how other people are idiots. So I try not to make assumptions and unnecessary interpretations any more. I have a little mantra I say to myself to help with this: "I don't really know what is going on here." Then I ask myself: "Is it going to cause me or anyone else bodily harm to wait a few extra seconds or minutes?" "Will anyone die over this?" The answer is—so far—always "no." So I calm myself down and I occupy my mind with this exercise. I try to imagine what MIGHT be going on with this person.

Once you have tried this exercise with a few imagined or remembered scenarios, try it in a real-life situation. Try it the next time you feel your ego get upset. Put yourself in the role of the person you are mad at. What would it take for YOU to do what they are doing? Try to tell a story so powerful that your heart shifts. This means the story has to be detailed and believable enough that IF it is true you really can see yourself doing that thing you are upset about.

EXERCISE 3: Developing an Attitude of Gratitude

If Reframing (Step 7 of the 9-step process) is the "meat and potatoes" of spiritual weightlifting, then gratitude is the dessert! And I love a good dessert.

After reframing a situation, I find it very helpful to move from the empathy and compassion I have triggered in myself by telling a new story to focusing on what I am grateful for in that moment (Step 8). In the car accident story, it is easy to be grateful for being alive and unharmed, able to go home and see my loved ones. I might also be grateful for being there to help others or for having enough money to have car insurance. In the express lane story I might be grateful that I have enough money to buy groceries at all or that I live in a country where food is plentiful and relatively cheap. I can be grateful that I know how to read or that I know how to shift my focus away from what is "wrong" in the situation to what is good so that I can feel compassion for others and experience positive emotions.

In almost any situation, you can find something to be grateful for—even it if is the strength you gain from surviving the problem, or the patience you are learning. You will get better at finding things to be grateful for the more you practice this skill.

A friend of mine told me once that he had a morning spiritual practice around gratitude. Every day while he drank his morning coffee, he would write in his journal three things he was grateful for. This doesn't sound difficult until you realize that his rule was he could never repeat something he'd written down before. Can you imagine? After 100 days (just over three months) you would have 300 different things in your journal that you were grateful for. What do you think a practice like this does to your mind and brain? You shift your focus. Instead of attending to what is "wrong" (the normal ego viewpoint) you start seeking what is RIGHT in the world—because you know you'll have to have three things to write tomorrow morning! You start to notice that beautiful flower along the sidewalk and note that you are grateful for that particular blossom. You notice how bright its petals are and how the yellow and pink blend together to make a gorgeous coral color. You notice how puffy and amazing the clouds are. You are grateful for the rain that nourished the plants. You see for the first time the lovely smile the cashier at the coffee shop flashes at customers and you are grateful for her kindness and good attitude. You savor your food and are grateful for the farmers who work so hard to make that meal possible for you, and for the truckers who bring it to your store, and to the produce manager or meat-department clerk who manages to keep it all cool and beautiful looking until you buy it and bring it home.

Gratitude is easy, fun, and changes the quality of your life in an instant. With practice it becomes a thick neural pathway—a habit. You start seeing what is right in the world easily, a very good antidote to the voice of the immature ego self. Gratitude is the voice of your Higher Self. And, like dessert, it tastes really good.

So go ahead and lift the heavy weights and reframe the situation (Step 7) to see with new eyes. Then reward yourself with the joy of gratitude (Step 8). From the reframe and gratitude steps you can then easily act with compassion and wisdom (step 9). As my buddy Jill likes to say, "lather, rinse, repeat." Keep it up, build up the spiritual muscle you need, and live a high-SQ life.

TWELVE

Deep Change, Infinite Impact

*"What vistas might we see if we were to understand
the full power of the human mind? The human
consciousness may prove the most inspiring frontier
in our history, an endless wellspring of knowledge,
and our means of liberation from all limitation. . . .
If we can find ways to awaken the full power of
awareness, we could enter a new phase of human
evolution and revitalize ourselves and our world."*

—Tarthang Tulku, *Knowledge of Freedom: Time to Change*

Around the time I started writing this book I also hired a team to help me rebrand my company, seeking to find a more authentic expression of my mission, purpose, and meaning. After much creative brainstorming and soul-searching, we came up with two words that captured for me the essence of what I am endeavoring to bring to my clients, my readers, the world, and the cosmos: Deep Change.

Deep change, to me, is the goal of SQ development. It's the kind of change that is sustainable, the impact of which is felt in ever-widening circles beyond the individual or organization who has undergone such a transformation. Deep change is evolutionary change—which means it represents a step beyond what has come before, rather than simply a modification of what already exists or a variation on an established theme. Authentic deep change can be the hardest kind of change to generate and sustain, but it also has the greatest impact.

Gary Hamel, a wise and innovative author who has been called by the *Wall Street Journal* "the world's most influential business thinker," observes that "there are two kinds of change: trivial and deep." Too often, he points out, "deep change is crisis-driven. People are pushed into the icy waters of change by circumstances outside of their control."

This is certainly true, whether in a business or in one's personal life. It is also true in political systems, cultures, and even in the natural world. Think of those moments when you have taken big leaps—and then look at what preceded them. Often it is moments of crisis that create space for change, breaking up the status quo that has previously existed and forcing innovation. However, I don't believe all deep change must be crisis-driven.

In my own life and work I have sought to find ways that individuals can consciously and deliberately engage in their own growth and transformation in order to evolve to a new level and impact the world around them in positive and evolutionary ways.

It seems to be human nature to resist change as long as possible. We have been conditioned since the dawn of our species to seek safety and security and to preserve the way things are as long as possible. It is often those who are leaders who are the most resistant to change because their power and position is all tied up in the status quo. What if we could change that? What if a new breed of spiritually intelligent leaders and change agents could show by example that it's not necessary for life to push us to the brink of disaster before we are willing to let go of our old ways of doing things, and create new ones? What if change became something we willingly embraced, and even sought out as it was called for? What if a calm, low-ego, and visionary approach, aligned with what was naturally trying to evolve or emerge, could inspire other people to enthusiastically engage with necessary change? And what if the new ways served humanity and our planet? I firmly believe that the leaders of the future will be those who develop this capacity. And the way I have found to develop this capacity is through cultivating the skillset I have described in this book: the skills of Spiritual Intelligence.

Of course, Spiritual Intelligence does not develop in a vacuum. As I described in Chapter 2, it is intimately connected with the other three key intelligences: Physical Intelligence (PQ), Cognitive Intelligence (IQ) and Emotional Intelligence (EQ). All of these intelligences need to be developed in order for deep change to be sustained, which is why I have started to refer to the sum total of these four as Deep Intelligence. The wisdom of Deep Intelligence will allow us not only to develop ourselves but to most effectively play the role we are here to play in the larger evolutionary process.

Evolution provides an important context for anyone who seeks to engage with their own growth and development in order to have an impact on those around them and the world we share. Since Charles Darwin published his revolutionary book in 1859, we have learned an extraordinary amount about where we have come from and where our cosmos has come from. As Brian Swimme and Mary Evelyn Tucker write in *The Journey of the Universe:*

> *We are the first generation to learn the comprehensive scientific dimensions of the universe story. We know that the observable universe emerged 13.7 billion years ago, and we now live on a planet orbiting our Sun, one of the trillions of stars in one of the billions of galaxies in an unfolding universe that is profoundly creative and interconnected. With our empirical observations expanded by modern science, we are now realizing that our universe is a single intense energy event that began as a tiny speck that has unfolded over time to become galaxies and stars, palms and pelicans, the music of Bach and each of us alive today. The great discovery of contemporary science is that the universe is not simply a place, but a story—a story in which we are immersed, to which we belong, and out of which we arose.*

If we contemplate it deeply, this new story can dramatically recontextualize the ways in which we think about our own lives, our own choices and actions, and our own development. It can help us to see our lives as connected to something larger, and to find a sense of deeper meaning and purpose. As I said at the opening of this book, being human is a great adventure—one that requires us to grow and stretch ourselves into fuller expression. The great French evolutionary mystic Pierre Teilhard de Chardin put it beautifully in his book *The Future of Man:*

> *Our fathers supposed themselves to go back no further than yesterday, each man containing within himself the ultimate value of his existence. They held themselves to be confined within the limits of their years on earth and their corporeal frame. We have blown asunder this narrow compass and those beliefs. At once humbled and ennobled by our discoveries, we are gradually coming to see ourselves as a part of vast and continuing*

> processes; as though awakening from a dream, we are begin-
> ning to realize that our nobility consists in serving, like intelligent
> atoms, the work proceeding in the Universe. We have discovered
> that there is a Whole, of which we are the elements. We have
> found the world in our own souls.

As "intelligent atoms" in the evolving, interconnected whole that is Life, we have reached a critical threshold in our development, one that requires all the wisdom and compassion we can muster if we are to move through it successfully. The challenges we face are multifaceted, complex, and systemic, and I would not for a moment claim to have "the solution." It will require the combined wisdom of many, many leaders and change agents coming from all walks of life, informed by different fields of expertise and life-experiences, to enable us to navigate the turbulent waters of today and tomorrow. But I do believe that Spiritual Intelligence can provide us with some important pieces of the puzzle. It offers common ground for people from many different religious faiths, as well as those who are not religious, to come together. Religious beliefs, as we know all too well, have often divided humanity and caused wars, oppression, and suffering. In the SQ21 I have, I hope, created a language that enables us to discuss these concepts without being limited to the language of any one faith tradition. These skills are in alignment with all the world's great wisdom traditions. The drive to optimize our human potential is a universal evolutionary pressure that spans cultures and faiths. As more and more of us develop our own SQ and share our discoveries, perhaps in a small but not insignificant way we can help to create greater understanding among the peoples of our planet.

The development of SQ will not only benefit individuals, it will also benefit their families, communities, and the companies they work for. Another goal of my work is that the faith-neutral language of competencies will make SQ acceptable for discussion in the workplace, which, after all, is the place where most of us spend most of our time. This will hopefully lead to support for individual and group SQ growth, creating more effective leaders, more meaningful work, improved products and services, and ensuring responsible corporate behavior. For my corporate clients who have engaged with SQ development, the personal and professional relevance has been clear.

In the end we are alike in our suffering, our hopes, and our joys. We are all striving to reach the same goals: less misery, and more peace, joy, and love. Perhaps with a more neutral language for SQ we can see our commonality and have a solid road map for the skill-building and capacity-building we need in order to get there.

Our evolving world is filled with beauty, with joy, and many good things, but few of us would argue that it is perfect. With eyes and hearts open, we can see not only our own suffering, but also the suffering of the world at large, including people of distant nations and ecosystems that struggle with the burden of toxins and other human-made change. We can passively sit and wish for a better world. But if everyone is passive, nothing will change. The deep change work of SQ may not be for everyone. As much as we might wish it for everyone, it may not be the work that everyone is willing to do. But for those of us who are courageous enough, who feel called to tackle the personal growth involved, the transformative potential is tremendous. And the potential for a better world grows with each person who takes on this work.

The circles of our impact go far beyond our awareness. The spiritual heroes we all feel so inspired by were/are each an individual like you and like me. We only have to look at their examples to see the impact that one person can have. You may not think of yourself as a Nelson Mandela or a Mother Teresa, but perhaps they did not think of themselves as global change agents either when they began to respond to the injustice or suffering they saw in front of them. Your individual growth and transformation can affect the world far more than you may realize now. We each make the differences we can make in the sphere of influence we have. And if our neighbors do the same, one after another, pretty soon we have not just a proverbial drop in the bucket. We have buckets and buckets of people making larger and larger waves in the ocean.

Tipping points are unpredictable, yet they do happen. A small but critical mass of people, by thinking and acting differently, created the European Renaissance. This renaissance period in Western history ushered in tremendous advances in philosophy, religion, art, and, especially, science. Today, open-minded thinkers continue to help us move forward by embracing science while, simultaneously, moving beyond the limitations of scientific materialism toward a more holistic understanding of what is real and how we can make sense of the world. The Conscious Capitalism movement is creating shifts in the reasons and the process for successful business. This new way of doing business factors in the interest of all the stakeholders, not just the owners/shareholders. And in the largest of human contexts, we are blessed in this era with the wisdom of the world being available to us through the easier travel, immigration that brings cultures together, and multiple electronic mediums of knowledge transfer. No longer are we constrained to learning from one philosophy, science, or faith tradition. We can feast on them all.

A banquet is wonderful, and tempting—and potentially distracting. So our task as individuals is to focus. "What do I need to learn or work on now?" I think of the SQ21 as one among many tools that can help us focus on what to develop, and how to develop it. And this matters not just for us as individuals, but for the human race and the ecosystems we impact.

Ultimately, the collective actions of the individuals who engage in the work of becoming fully human—developing their SQ along with their PQ, IQ, and EQ—will not only have enormous value for them, but it will have infinite impact on this precious blue-green planet we call Earth. We are all part of a miraculous, ever-evolving whole.

As a capstone intelligence, I believe that SQ amplifies and guides the other intelligences. This gives it special value as a high-leverage set of skills to improve our personal lives and our leadership capacity. We can each do our part by developing our intelligences, until the tipping point is reached. Small actions can lead to infinite impact. Take your next Spiritual Intelligence skill-development step now, and begin the joyful process of living into your full humanity and potential.

APPENDIX 1

How the SQ21 was Created and Researched

This is a non-technical summary of the process we went through to create the SQ21 and to validate it. If you would like a more technical and detailed document, please go to www.deepchange.com and look under "Dig Deeper."

History

When I began this journey I knew that I wanted to create something more concrete and useful than anything I could find in the spiritual domain. Initially, I struggled with how to start. In my gut, I felt that SQ as an intelligence would be similar to but more difficult than EQ—a vertical step up. My favorite model of EQ, by Daniel Goleman and Richard Boyatzis, had four quadrants.

Self-Awareness	Social Awareness or Other Awareness
Self-Management	Social Skills or Relationship Skills

So I began by drawing a parallel four quadrants and imagining what might go in them. What would the quadrant headers be? The first pass looked something like this:

Higher Self-Awareness	Awareness of all that is (seeing below the surface)
Living in alignment with Higher Self	How others perceive me, how I live

Since I had come to the conclusion that a foundation concept in SQ was the ability to shift from ego to Higher Self, I decided to name the upper left quadrant "Awareness of Ego Self and Higher Self." Then I thought about the skills that would comprise that. What would be needed to be aware of your Higher Self? I frequently referred to the spiritual exemplars we tend to admire. I would run through them mentally—what would the Dalai Lama have as a skill-set? Mother Teresa? Gandhi? And so on.

After much thinking, I got to the 21 skills. I kept trying to consolidate down to 20 so it would be "tidy"—five per quadrant. But it didn't seem to work, so I left it alone.

At this point I hired outside experts, Dr. Brant Wilson and his business partner, Joan E. Jones, to help me design the survey itself. They guided me as I worked to create the assessment questions.

First came the hard work of describing the twenty-one skills, from novice to expert levels. I was hoping to find four levels of each—again, thinking about my model in relationship to the Emotional Competence Inventory by Boyatzis and Goleman that has four levels per skill. I was also thinking about the spiritual exemplars, and about the Stages of Faith model by James Fowler. As I worked through each skill, they all seemed to fall into five levels, not four. So I finally gave up my desire to have four levels and went with what felt more natural. Later, as I studied the work of Susanne Cook-Greuter and other developmental psychologists, I came to understand the five levels were corresponding roughly not only with Fowler's stages of faith, but also with the levels of adult development. In any event, five seemed to be what fit.

The Alpha Pilot

I had the joy of both a focus group process and an alpha pilot process, thanks to the help of Dr. Judith Neal, who was then heading the Association for Spirit at Work, and is now the executive director of the Tyson Center for Faith and Spirituality in the Workplace. She helped me pull together a group of coaches and consultants who were trying to find a safe and effective way to integrate spirituality into workplace conversations. These volunteers agreed to work through my first version of the skills and levels and take the alpha version of the survey. We worked through one quadrant at a time, and they gave me feedback on how I described the levels, and whether or not I had them in the right order, or had left anything out. They took the first version of the survey and commented on the questions and the scoring method. I am deeply grateful to Judi and all of those in that first group for their help.

Based on their feedback, we made clarifications to the language, added a popup glossary to the survey, and improved the scoring and reporting process. Then we launched into testing the assessment.

What Makes a Strong Assessment?

There is no perfection where self-assessments are concerned. People can overstate or understate their own abilities. But there are ways to make self-assessments sound enough to be truly useful. These include:

- Build the questions based on best practices for wording questions. For example, use focus groups to check your word choices. And test only one construct per question. Experts in survey creation assisted us in this regard.

- Use scales that are respected, such as the "Likert Scale," a 1 to 5 scale in our case where people agree on whether they do something (rating themselves from "not at all" to "completely" on various questions,) or comment on how frequently they do something (rating themselves from "never" to "consistently"). We use Likert Scales on almost all the survey questions. We have one yes/no question and one multiple choice.

- Mix up the scoring system to avoid people just answering down one side of the scales. We have designed the SQ21 survey so that higher-scoring answers are sometimes to the right, sometimes to the left, sometimes in the middle.

The Beta Pilot

In late 2003/early 2004 we offered the survey to as many people as we could find who were willing to take it. More than five hundred people participated. The survey allowed space at the end for feedback and questions. And the respectable number of participants allowed us to do some reliability studies. The internal reliability of the assessment was shown to be very high. A few words were still causing some confusion, and we struggled with a few questions that didn't seem quite right yet.

The World Business Academy

Approximately one hundred people attending the 2004 World Business Academy conference participated in the SQ21 development by taking the survey and giving us feedback on the language. After this, we made a few more minor changes and considered the assessment "ready for prime time." Many thanks to Rinaldo Brutoco for making this work possible.

Additional Research

In 2006, a study done at the University of North Texas, under supervision by Dr. Michael McElhenie, evaluated the scores people got on the SQ21 and compared those results to how they answered questions either by essay or by interview. The intention was to assess if the SQ21 scores were reflective of what the graduate students were seeing in the essays and interviews. In other words—was the SQ21 measuring what we thought it was measuring? The answer was yes. This is called **Criterion Validity** (more on that below).

In 2008, with help from Dr. Susanne Cook-Greuter, Dr. Brant Wilson, and Joan E. Jones, a study was completed testing a key hypothesis related to the value of the SQ21. This hypothesis was that higher scores on the SQ21 would be highly correlated to (related to) higher scores on a respected model of stages of adult development. We did in fact find a strong positive relationship between stages of adult development as measured by an assessment called the SCTi-MAP and the SQ21 scores. This was an important step in demonstrating the value of the SQ21 for leaders, as higher stages of adult development have been linked to the ability to deal with complexity, ambiguity, and rapid change, as well as to the ability to successfully navigate transformational change in businesses.[46] This is an important test of one construct of my theory, so it is said to provide some **Construct Validity** (more below).

Future Research

There are an almost infinite numbers of potential research projects that could improve our understanding of SQ and how to develop it. If you are interested in doing research with the SQ21, please contact Deep Change.

Frequently Asked Questions Regarding the Validity and Reliability of the SQ21

Was this tool expertly created?

Yes. Well-trained people with expertise in survey creation assisted in the development of this assessment, including discussing constructs, question wording, and developing the scoring system.

Reliability: Is there an expected level of internal consistency?

There is a statistical measure known as Cronbach's alpha. It is a measure of internal consistency. It answers the question, "Are the related items in the survey showing a strong relationship to each other?" When items are measuring a similar construct, they should be yielding results that are positively related. The alpha from the Beta Pilot study was .97 (which is exceptionally high).

Validity: Does the test measure what it claims to measure?

From an academic perspective, validity is complex and essentially you are never done testing and improving a survey. However, you can show reasonable validity for an assessment in the following ways.

- Face validity: the questions should "make sense to people" as being related to the content you are claiming to measure. And the report showing how people scored and suggesting next steps should make sense to the client and to people who know him/her well as being a reasonable reflection of the person. The SQ21 consistently receives strong positive feedback from clients and coaches for face validity.

- Criterion validity: does the assessment measure what it claims to measure? A 2006 study by a graduate student at the University of North Texas, supervised by Dr. Michael McElhenie, showed that the SQ21 results, when compared to essays and/or interviews of the research subjects, yielded results that aligned positively. The SQ21 does seem to measure what it claims to measure.

- Construct validity: do the assessment results align with the theory it puts forward? For example, by 2005, I had hypothesized that SQ is an intelligence that is supportive of and perhaps even required for higher stages of adult development. If a theory claims that when A goes up B will go up, then construct validity asks does that hold true when tested? One test of my hypothesis was done in 2008 when we looked at 139 subjects who took both the SQ21 and a respected measure of stages of adult development—the SCTi/MAP by Dr Susanne Cook-Greuter. A high correlation was, in fact, found between higher stages of adult development and higher scores on the SQ21. Dr. Brant Wilson described the result as a 1% chance that this relationship is an accident. Proving correlation is not the same as causation—so further study is needed to see if SQ development can act as an accelerant of adult development, and/or if the failure to develop SQ skills impedes development. This would have great relevance for leadership development, as well as for personal growth.

Overall, I can say with confidence that the SQ21 is a solid tool. It meets or exceeds the required expectations of the clients and companies I have worked with.

That being said, I will add what I tell all the coaches I train: It is an assessment designed to begin a conversation and a learning journey. It is not perfect. But it's really good as a starting place for one of the richest conversations you might ever have with a coach, or with yourself.

ENDNOTES

1 Later renamed ExxonMobil after the merger with Mobil Corporation.

2 Covey, Stephen, "Principled Communication," article published on www.franklincovey.com, © 1996, 1998 Covey Leadership Center and Franklin Covey.

3 See http://www.vetta.org/definitions-of-intelligence/.

4 Sternberg, R. J., quoted in R. L. Gregory, *The Oxford Companion to the Mind* (Oxford, UK: Oxford University Press, 1998).

5 Gardner, Howard, *A Multiplicity of Intelligences,* published in the Scientific American, 1998.

6 Quoted in Hoffman, Edward, *The Right to Be Human: A Biography of Abraham Maslow,* (McGraw-Hill, 1999) p. 143.

7 Goleman, Daniel, "What Makes a Leader?" *Harvard Business Review,* 1998, reprinted in Best of HBR, 2004.

8 Brooks, David, "Amy Chua Is a Wimp," *New York Times,* January 18, 2011, p. A25.

9 Zohar, Danah, and Marshall, Ian, *SQ: The Ultimate Intelligence,* p. 276.

10 Gardner, Howard, "A Case Against Spiritual Intelligence," *The International Journal for the Psychology of Religion,* Volume 10, Issue 1 January 2000, pp. 27-34.

11 Gardner, Howard, *Intelligence Reframed: Multiple Intelligences for the 21st Century* (Basic Books, 1999) p. 53.

12 Covey, Stephen, *The 8th Habit: From Effectiveness to Greatness* (Simon and Schuster, 2004) p. 53.

13 Wilber, Ken, *Eye to Eye: The Quest for the New Paradigm* (Shambhala, 2001) ch.3.

14 Seneca, Letter 71, *Selected Philosophical Letters,* trans. Brad Inwood (New York, N.Y.: Oxford University Press, 2007), p. 25.

15 For a more detailed description of the creation and validation of the SQ21, see Appendix 1, p. 189.

16 Goleman and Boyatzis prefer the abbreviation "EI" for emotional intelligence. I am sticking with the "Q" abbreviations (IQ, EQ, PQ, SQ) that are very popular and help people make the connection with multiple intelligences, beginning with IQ.

17 Dr. Neal at the time was the founder and executive director of the Association for Spirit at Work. She also founded the Willis Harman Spirit at Work Awards. She is the author of *Edgewalkers* and is currently the Executive Director of the Tyson Center for Faith and Spirituality in the Workplace at the University of Arkansas.

18 See www.valuescentre.com for more on Richard Barrett's fabulous assessment tools.

19 If you are interested in learning about the SQ21 in greater detail, the first step is to take the assessment yourself, which you can do at www.deepchange.com.

20 Wright, N. T., *The New Testament and the People of God,* (Fortress Press, September 1992) p. 125.

21 Wilber, Ken, in "God's Playing a New Game," in *What Is Enlightenment?* Magazine, issue 33 (June-August 2006).

22 The Myers-Briggs Type Indicator was developed by Katharine Briggs and Isabel Briggs Myers. It is based on the psychological theory of Carl Jung. It measures our innate preferences on 4 scales: Introversion/Extroversion; Sensing/Intuiting; Thinking/Feeling and Judging/Perceiving. For more information, go to www.cpp.com.

23 Maslow, Abraham, *Motivation and Personality,* (New York: Harper and Row, 1954) p. 91.

24 Business author Jim Collins has written about the importance of this skill for the higher levels of leadership, specifically for what he calls Level 5 leadership. He calls it "both/and thinking." Both/and thinking has to do with the ability to not get locked in the either/or. Either/or thinking tends to be "it's my way or the highway," and there tend to be limitations to the creativity of either/or thinking. Both/and thinkers find much more creative solutions.

25 See the work of Susanne Cook-Greuter, Robert Kegan, Bill Torbert and others.

26 For more on stages of ego development see the work of Robert Kegan, Susanne Cook-Greuter, Bill Torbert, or Bill Joiner.

27 Einstein, Albert, Letter to Robert S. Marcus, February 12, 1950, in *Dear Professor Einstein,* Ed. Alice Calaprice (New York: Prometheus Books, 2002) p. 184.

28 Dr. Martin Luther King Jr., "Letter from the Birmingham Jail," on the website of the Martin Luther King, Jr., Research and Education Institute: http://mlkkpp01.stanford.edu/index.php/encyclopedia/encyclopedia/enc_letter_from_birmingham_jail_1963/.

29 ScienceDaily, July 31, 2007.

30 There are many on the Internet—check out especially those at www.mindfake.com.

31 See http://www.pbs.org/wnet/brain/illusions/index.html.

32 Wilber, Ken, *A Brief History of Everything* (Shambhala Press, 2001), pp. 42-43.

33 Huxley, Aldous, *The Perennial Philosophy* (HarperCollins, July 1990) p. xi.

34 From the 2007 documentary *In the Shadow of the Moon* (Discovery Films, Film Four).

35 James, William, *Varieties of Religious Experience* (Touchstone: 1997) p. 379.

36 Vaillant, George, *Spiritual Evolution: A Scientific Defense of Faith* (Harmony, 2008), p. 8.

37 Ibid., p. 9.

38 Ibid., p. 14.

39 Ibid., p. 17.

40 Daniel Goleman, *Destructive Emotions* (Bantam, January 1, 2003), p.3.

41 Dr. Larry Stockman and Cynthia S. Graves (my name at that time), *Grown-Up Children Who Won't Grow Up.* (Prima Lifestyles, 1990, 1994).

42 For more on this see David Emerald's wonderful book, *The Power of TED,* about the drama triangle (victim, hero and persecutor) and how to move to "The Empowerment Dynamic" or "TED."

43 It is a beautiful exercise to have someone reflect your highest aspirations back to you. It reflects the yearning of your Higher Self to be all you have come here to be. Sometimes clients get very choked up when they see the beauty of this side of themselves. Taking time to deeply see this virtuous side of you is related to Skills 2, 3 and 4.

44 Peck, M. Scott, *The Road Less Traveled,* (Touchstone, 1978/1992), p. 85.

45 See the Deep Change website for a full resource directory to support your skill development.

46 See Rooke, David and Torbert, William R., "Seven Transformations of Leadership" in *Harvard Business Review,* April 2005.

GLOSSARY OF
SQ-RELATED TERMS

Belief System: A worldview (see definition of worldview below) that explains the origin of the universe, how to live a good life, and the meaning of life. Everyone participates in a belief system, whether it is a traditional religion, a secular worldview, or something else. Once this is made conscious, we can choose to adopt a belief system that fosters the growth of our spiritual intelligence.

Ego or Ego self: The sense of being a separate, individual person; the process of making meaning in the world; and the part of us that is self-concerned. The ego is an integral part of the human being because it helps us to fulfill our basic human physical and emotional needs, but it is still only a part of the totality of who we are. When we live primarily from the ego we often feel and act with selfishness, fear, or anger. Spiritual development includes realizing that our identities include more than the ego and replacing harmful egoic patterns of thought, feeling, and behavior with healthier egoic patterns that work with the Higher Self. *Synonyms: personal self, personality self, separate self, small self.*

The Golden Rule: "Do unto others as you would have them do unto you." This rule appears in some form in all major religious traditions and in many philosophies. Sometimes it is stated in the reverse: "Do not do unto others as you would not have them do unto you."

Higher Power: The energy and intelligence behind the manifest world— the flow of what is, the Tao. It is something "larger than me" that is noble or sacred. What you consider to be a description of "Higher Power" may not be what others would agree with, so tolerance for synonyms is important. *Synonyms: all that is, everything, life itself, being, love,* nature, the universe, or ultimate reality; and from some religious traditions: God, Goddess, Emptiness, Allah, YHWH, Jehovah, Ein Sof, Brahman, Spirit or Great Spirit, the Tao, the Divine.

Higher Self: The part of ourselves that is unselfish, loving, and wise; our inner voice of wisdom and universal concern that sees that there is no absolute distinction between "me" and "others." We act from our Higher Selves when we are inspired by our vision of the Higher Power. Synonyms: inner wisdom, authentic self, spirit self, essence, true self; and from some religious traditions: the light of the Divine within me, Christ consciousness, Buddha-nature, Atman.

Integrity: Honesty, truthfulness, authenticity: "I walk my talk." Aligning our words and actions to the values of our Higher Self.

Intelligence: The ability to respond skillfully in real situations. A latent aptitude, such as a natural talent for music, does not become "musical intelligence" until you study and practice and develop the skill to actually play music well. Similarly, we are all spiritual beings, but we are not all spiritually intelligent until we study and practice and develop our spiritual skills.

Intuition: Knowing something and yet not necessarily knowing how you know it. Synonyms: hunch, gut feeling, body-sense, direct knowing, direct experience, insight, inner wisdom.

Larger Reality/Larger Perspective: Since the human perceptual process is limited, a fully inclusive perspective on what is real includes that which human eyes may not be able to see. With regards to spiritual development, adopting a larger perspective requires learning to see beyond the surface of things through intuition, spiritual insight, and grace. Our understanding of ourselves and the world expands through spiritual practices such as prayer or meditation, and with the help of our community, teachers, and experts.

Mission: Based on the values of your Higher Self, your Mission explains how you wish to contribute to the world. Synonyms: life's work, life purpose, calling, higher purpose, vocation, reason for being, personal contribution to the world.

Mysticism: The pursuit of communion with, identity with, or conscious awareness of an ultimate reality, spiritual truth, or God through direct experience, intuition, or insight. In Islam, the Sufi tradition is the mystical branch. In Judaism, it is Kabbalah. In Christianity it occurs in multiple denominations as the journey through the Dark Night of the Soul to "The Cloud of Unknowing." Eastern religions have well-developed traditions of mystical practice as well. Mystical states of consciousness can also be developed outside the context of traditional religions. For example, contemplation of nature or various types of secular meditation can have similar results to religious mystical practices.

Nonjudgmental: Keeping an open mind and heart. Being deeply understanding while maintaining discernment and the ability to take appropriate action as needed. At the highest level of compassion and non-judgment, we see that we too might share another person's thoughts, beliefs, emotions and behaviors if we were in his or her situation. This enables wise and compassionate responses.

Peak Experiences: There are many different types of peak experiences, but they are all temporary. Peak experiences feel "different" from everyday perception, often involving a moment of awe and wonder, an expanded sense of self beyond the ego, or a feeling of timelessness. Some people report that colors are much more vivid and that everything—rocks, trees, clouds—seems "alive." There is often a sense of profound peace and joy, and a sense that "everything is okay." A sense of deep compassion for and connection to all living things often arises in such moments, a sense of being connected to, a part of, or "at one" with everything. Sometimes people may feel transported outside of their bodies and sense themselves as consciousness or spirit, independent of physical form. After a peak experience, it can feel a bit depressing or limiting to "snap back" into ordinary experiences.

Religion: A faith tradition; a specific set of teachings, beliefs, rituals, and practices that belong to a group of people. These teachings and practices are designed to help the seeker relate appropriately with a divinity or ultimate reality. They will typically teach how to live an ethical life; usually there is a founder and a sacred text(s). Most of the major religions have subgroups, or denominations. For example, within Christianity, Roman Catholics, Greek Orthodox, and Anglicans are just three of the hundreds of denominations. See the related definition "Spirituality" below and "Belief System" above.

Spirituality: The human need to be in connection with something larger than our ego self, something sacred and timeless. Spirituality may be expressed through religion or it may not. Spirituality contributes to a fulfilling life and manifests in two ways: (1) a "vertical" desire to be in relationship with the Higher Power and (2) a "horizontal" desire to be of service to other people, creatures, or the planet.

Spiritual Laws/Universal Truths/Spiritual Principles: Spiritual guidelines, rules, teachings, or ideas that explain the right way to live, how human beings can achieve happiness and inner peace, how our inner life shapes our experiences, or how things work in the world. Examples: "As you give to others, so you will receive," or, "What you believe is what you will create." Spiritual principles are different from the laws of physics in that we cannot, at this time, easily measure them in typical scientific ways. Yet we can experiment with them in our own lives and see if they appear to work as taught. For example: Do moral behaviors create better relationships and more inner peace? The SQ21 model identifies two levels of spiritual laws: (1) simpler ones like the Golden Rule or various ethical teachings that explain what to *do* in the world and (2) more complex ones that explain how to *be* in the world, such as "live in the ever-present moment of Now," or "what I focus on expands." *Synonyms: sage advice, life lessons.*

Suffering: Mental or emotional distress. Suffering is often created by our resistance to what is. We resist unchangeable facts (like our age) or we resist what is happening around us or to us. Suffering is somewhat avoidable, while pain, which is biological or neurological, may not be. Some challenges in life are inevitable. We can meet these challenges more effectively by not getting lost in upset (optional suffering). When we do experience pain or suffering, we can turn it to good through developing compassion for ourselves and others.

Transcendent Timelessness: The experience of stepping out of our normal perceptions of time and change and into the perception of eternity, or that which never changes and is free of our normal limitations. Paradoxically, this may also feel like being totally present in the now.

Transcendent Timelessness may be one aspect of a Peak Experience, or it may be more stable. Repeated familiarization with this perception can dramatically alter our sense of ourselves and our relationship to life.

Values: Things, qualities, or principles that are important to us and that influence the decisions and actions we take. Examples: family, health, work, success, honesty, trustworthiness, humility, piety, loyalty, generosity, devotion.

Worldview: This literally means "the way I see the world." Any worldview is made up of what we believe is "right" or "wrong," how we think things "should be," and what we think is true and false. People may agree with all, some, or none of someone else's worldview. Worldviews are shared by communities of people and based partly on geography, religion, age, culture, nationality, level of education, life experiences, and biological realities such as how our brains work. Our worldview profoundly affects our perception of reality. We filter all the data we receive through our senses and through our Worldview so that we can make sense of it. Our filters inherently "leave stuff out" (especially what we don't understand or don't want to see), so each worldview excludes some information. Worldviews also "add stuff" by interpreting and making meaning out of what is being observed. Thus, by leaving out and adding in, each of us can reach amazingly different interpretations of the same events. Worldviews, once made conscious, can be adjusted to be as accurate as possible. *Synonyms: philosophy of life, belief system, personal filters, lens through which I see the world, my window on the world.*

Recommended Further Reading on Multiple Intelligences and Leadership

HOWARD GARDNER

Frames of Mind: The Theory of Multiple Intelligences
Intelligence Reframed: Multiple Intelligences for the 21st Century

DANIEL GOLEMAN

Emotional Intelligence: Why It Can Matter More Than IQ
(10th Anniversary Edition)
Working With Emotional Intelligence
Social Intelligence: The New Science of Human Relationships
Destructive Emotions: A Scientific Dialogue with the Dalai Lama

With RICHARD BOYATZIS and ANNIE MCKEE

Primal Leadership: Learning to Lead with Emotional Intelligence
Primal Leadership: The Hidden Driver of Great Performance

RICHARD BOYATZIS and ANNIE MCKEE

Resonant Leadership: Renewing Yourself and Connecting with Others Through Mindfulness, Hope, and Compassion

KEN WILBER

Integral Psychology: Consciousness, Spirit, Psychology, Therapy

INDEX

INDEX by Skill

INDEX

To learn more about Cindy Wigglesworth and Spiritual Intelligence, take the SQ21 Assessment, and find resources for developing the 21 Skills, please visit

www.deepchange.com